Under Milk Wood
by Dylan Thomas

Andrew Sinclair

Screenplay by
Andrew Sinclair

Timon Films

This edition published in 2014 by Timon Films Limited,
Flat 20 Millenium House,
132 Grosvenor Road, London, SW1V 3JY

ISBN 978-0-9576885-0-6

Printed in Great Britain and distributed by Witley Press Ltd,
24-26 Greevegate, Hunstanton, Norfolk, PE36 6AD
Email: bookshop@witleypress.co.uk
Website: www.witleypress.co.uk

Distribution and sales: Reel Solutions, Dean Clough,
Halifax, HX3 5AX
Website: www.reelsolutions.co.uk
www.undermilkwoodfilm.com

MILK WOOD AND MAGIC
by Andrew Sinclair

There is a law in making a decent film in this country. The law is, the impossible must always happen. That is why so few decent films can be made over here, although Britain is full of good film-makers.

The impossible always happened in making *Under Milk Wood.* At times, its luck exceeded incredulity and vanished into Celtic mist. Like a necromancer juggling the elements, any Merlin of the screen has to mix the gold of the backers with the stars in their courses and come up with a horoscope that guarantees fair heavens and a safe return. To go at all, *Under Milk Wood* had to find a time when Richard Burton, Elizabeth Taylor, and Peter O'Toole were all available to work and in this island, which was rather like fixing a week-end between Howard Hughes, Elizabeth the Second and Puck. Then the gold had to be conjured in double-quick time from the state and a merchant bank, both of whom were rightly foolish enough to buck the wisdom of Wardour Street and think there could be profit as well as art in the wild warm words of that people's poet, Dylan Thomas. Then there had to be hayfield sun in March in Fishguard, which would be a blessing not seen in thirty years. ("*Wales* in winter!" said the drenched warriors streaming home from Polanski's protracted *Macbeth.* "Jesus ! Not only did Banquo blow off his horse, but the bloody horse blew away too.") Then we had a forty days' budget about as fat as Our Lord's when he had the same schedule in the wilderness. What with sixty sets and seventy actors, we had to spend a quarter of our time just shifting from scene to scene; we shot on the run, with the mighty heroes of Lee Electrics humping the hundredweight brute lights as casually as kittens on their shoulders. Everything and everyone had to work too well, beyond normal and halfway to dream. The technicians would mutter about "Andrew the Luck." And I would answer, "Miracles happen daily." Frankly they had to, so they did.

There is a necessity in a film, once it has begun, which matches the resignation in a Celt, once he has decided to go for broke. There are so many shots to be taken each day, so many actors to play their scenes while they are still available, so many seconds of film to be put successfully in the can each week - or else, the boot. Considerations of art come a bad second to sheer endurance. One makes the script and hopes it works. Any improvisation on the set is a dangerous gift that may save the part, but throw the whole. The important thing, as Beckett once wrote, is to be done, to have done. And to have done well.

For there are no excuses. A film-maker is judged by the final film. He can plead none of his troubles on the way, too little time, bad weather, fractious actors, intervention from the money, accident. But then he gets the credit for the greatness of the others' performance. In *Under Milk Wood,* that ultimate professional O'Toole insisted on wearing milky-blue contact lenses that covered his whole eye-ball to play the blind Captain Cat. The trouble was that he could only stand the lenses in his eyes for half-an-hour at a whack, and then he was really going blind after four days of it. If he had not been such a superb performer capable of five-minute takes hitting an unseen mark without a wrong word, we could never have completed his shots on schedule with him still seeing. As it was, the courage of the man lasted far beyond the good of his eyes until the last four longish shots, which we took from the back or with his lids closed.

Yet endurance and luck are not enough to make a good film. There has to be magic as well. And magic is not on call. For me, *Under Milk Wood* has always been the supreme incantation of my life. However many hundred times I hear the words during the tedious repetitions of editing and dubbing a film, the phrases still reverberate and comfort and tease meanings as only the great sentences do. Richard Burton would complain of being woken o'nights by voices haunting him with Dylan's words; but his own voice with its fits and starts, graduations and gravels, choirs and harmonies is the midnight speech of the lost Bards of Wales. The magic began when he recorded the sullen craft of his dead friend's words all in two hours in a Soho cellar before the picture started. We always had that spell to play back to ourselves during the bad days, and every time we heard it, the magic came again and we thought that *Under Milk Wood* might work after all.

Daring to make a classic like Dylan's is a fool's leap into the dark wood. The arrogance of setting forth one's own visual imagination on a screen to compete with the dreams of the many followers of the poet with their own dark-bright visions from the words alone invites the destruction of the gods. Yet our insolence somehow seemed to amuse the Welsh gods. If they did not forgive us, they played with us obscurely, and through their fatal teasing, they brought the magic into the film. If I can try to describe what is beyond sense. . .

The problem of *Under Milk Wood* as a film lay in its bittiness, cross-cutting from voice to voice all the time without knowing whose voice it was. Seventy little stories to tell in ninety minutes in the life of a small fishing-port. The connecting link Two Voices, their characters and connection with the town unexplained, Voices with the power to conjure up dreams, knowing intimately the private lives of all the sleepers in Cockle Row and Coronation Street, godlike in their comprehension and devilish in their mockery. How to make this counterpoint of words into one visual whole, while being faithful to the text. . . It was daunting.

I had only half-solved the problem when we began shooting the film. I had given the two Voices faces and characters, pre-dominance to the powerful, brooding face and pale-piercing eyes of Richard Burton, foolery to the thin, playful, melancholic skull's head of Ryan Davies, the beloved clown of Welsh television, playing the jester to Burton's King, the imp to Lucifer. I had gone back to an early experience of Dylan's, when he had spent a weekend with a friend in Gower, and the friend's girl with a loose red mouth had swapped beds. I had also gone back to Dylan's other great radio play, *"Return Journey,"* where the old Dylan travels home to look for the young Dylan, and the final refrain is the same as in Polly Garter's song . . . "dead, dead, dead." There was also a story of his called *"Just Like Little Dogs,"* where two men take out two sisters on the beach and the girls change partners in the night. So I made the reason for the two Voices going back to Llaregyb their quest for a girl, Norma Jane Jenkins, whom they had met way back in the war, and had shared; it made for nice intercutting with the children's kissing games, Billy and Johnnie Cristo and Dicky kissing Gwennie, and with Polly Garter's song as she scrubs the floor of the Welfare Hall.

"Tom, Dick, and Harry were three fine men
And I'll never have such loving again. . . ."

Then Norma Jane walks away into a graveyard and the men leave town in their khaki coats, and it is revealed that Norma Jane had been dead a long time, and that these two visible spirits from the sea and the dark wood have come back to relive their life in the timeless town and resurrect their lost love.

This device gave a unity to the film, a visual reason for all the marvellous speeches of the Voices, that orchestration of words which makes *Under Milk Wood* as binding as a spell. But it did not solve the problem of the final coming together of the townspeople, nor did it help the dying fall of the picture, which trailed away into nothing. But we do not always make movies. Sometimes movies make us.

We were filming the night shot of Evans the Death, the undertaker, asleep by an open coffin, laughing in his dreams. The undertaker's shop had been built by us in front of two lavatories on the quayside of Lower Fishguard, which otherwise served naturally as Cockle Row. We had set up the shot through the window of the shop on the first three letters FUN from FUNERALS - beyond the glass, the end of the bed, with Evans the Death's toes curling through a hole in his purple socks. Then a coastguard siren wailed behind us, meaning trouble at sea. And policemen hurried up the quayside, and we stopped work, and a boat set out across the bay. And we looked at the cliffs opposite until the boat came back. In it, the body of a drowned boy. One of our electricians thought it was the body of his child, and he broke down. It turned out to be the child of a local free-lance cameraman, who normally worked for television. But in the dead child, we all saw our own deaths and the deaths of our children. So we packed up and went home till the morning.

The funeral was two days later. So I and the Associate Producer left the scene of Polly Garter singing, "Little Willy Wee is dead, dead, dead . . .", to pay our respects to the family of the boy and leave wreaths from the company. The father met us, a brave and good man. He said he would not find it easy to leave overnight his wife and other children and his home for some weeks now. So we offered him work in getting us some shots of seals, which we might need. For he knew where the seals were at this time of year.

What we did not know was that the seals lay at the bottom of a thousand foot cliff. Putting his Arrifiex on his back, the brave cameraman and two of our party got down that cliff, risking their lives and losing the top of a finger. The father came back with some spectacular shots, including one of a group of seals humping away into the foam.

We went back next week and did the shot of the undertaker laughing by the coffin, although nobody wanted to think of it. Dylan had written it, and it still had to be done. But when I saw the rushes of the seals and I reread *Under Milk Wood* for the hundredth time, I saw where the magic and the end of the picture lay. Celtic myths are full of seals coming back from the sea; their singing voices are meant to be the drowned dead, like the five sailors who come back to Captain Cat in his dreams. "I lost my step in Nantucket," says Dancing Williams, now down salt deep into the Davy dark. And endlessly, Dylan refers to dreams coming from the black sea. . .

> *"Only you can hear and see, behind the eyes of the sleepers, the flight and fall and despairs and big seas of their dreams. . ."*
>
> *"Now behind the eyes and secrets of the dreamers in the streets rocked to sleep by the sea, see the .. wrecks and sprats and shells and fishbones, whale juice and moonshine and small salt fry dished up by the hidden sea."*

So I filmed a night dream dance in the pouring rain, with a gale blowing the roofs away, while the actors playing the people of Llarregyb caracoled around the town pump and danced away into the sea, and they were dissolved into seals, and Satan's jester walked back from the wild drowned caper he had led from the back of a squealing pig to the black Milk Wood, where the Devil of Richard Burton was waiting, crossing himself and smiling darkly, with his last incantation sounding, that begins

> *"The Wood, whose every tree- foot's cloven in the black glad sight of the hunters of lovers. . ."*

And *Under Milk Wood* had an end, a magical end, that had grown out of its words and its making, out of the life of the welcoming town and the death of the boy that had its sad meaning to us all, out of the rich deep words of the Welsh poet of poets and the tears in Captain Cat's eyes as he remembers Rosie Probert and his lost sailoring days

> *"Seas barking like seals,*
> *Blue seas and green,*
> *Seas covered with eels*
> *And mermen and whales."*

Richard Burton had said to me that *Under Milk Wood* was all about religion, sex and death, and I did not understand his words until the film was over. My preacher and teacher was not the fond-foolish Reverend Eli Jenkins nor the dark Puritan Jack Black from Dylan's text, but my dandy-dark cameraman Bob Huke, who made me watch the twilights away in his quest for that one shot at evening which he called "the magic hour." And in that "dusk and ceremonial dust, and night's first darkening snow," I sensed the timeless powers of the Gwaun Valley, where the pagan stones still stand at the doorways and the mistletoe hangs from the wind-bent oaks, the powers of light and night, wind and water, stone and hill, crow and cromlech, Celtic cross and bleeding yew, which are still the old gods in that Pembrokeshire where the ancient Celts quarried stones to drag all the way to Stonehenge. And I knew that we only had to resign ourselves to the place and its doings to recapture the spell of Dylan's words and describe Milk waking Wood.

If *Under Milk Wood* works as a film, it will be because we were all the servants of the dead Dylan Thomas, who caught the essence of all Welsh sea-towns and made an incantation of them. The film was the making of us. We were not making the film.

CREDITS :

Screenplay by	Andrew Sinclair
from the original play	
Under Milk Wood by	Dylan Thomas
Directed by	Andrew Sinclair
Executive Producers	Jules Buck and Hugh French
Production Company	Timon Films Ltd.
Associate Producer	John Comfort
Music composed by	Brian Gascoigne
Welsh folk songs sung by	Bryn Williams and Olwen Rees
Director of Photography	Bob Huke
Art Director	Geoffrey Tozer
Camera Operator	Dennis Lewiston
First Assistant Director	Dominic Fulford
Second Assistant Director	Bob Howard
Continuity	Ann Skinner
Editor	Willy Kemplen
Assistant Editors	Peter Davies and Les Healey
Sound Mixer	Cyril Collick
Dubbing Editor	John Poyner
Make-up	Eric Allwright
Hairdresser	Joan White
Wardrobe	Dulcie Midwinter
Location Designer	Jacquemine Charrott-Lodwidge

Under Milk Wood was chosen to open the Venice Film Festival in 1971

CAST:

First Voice	Richard Burton
Rosie Probert	Elizabeth Taylor
Captain Cat	Peter O'Toole
Myfanwy Price	Glynis Johns

Nogood Boyo	David Jason
Mrs. Pugh	Vivien Merchant
Mrs. Ogmore-Pritchard	Sian Phillips
Second Voice	Ryan Davies
Mog Edwards	Victor Spinetti
Gossamer Beynon	Angharad Rees
Polly Garter	Ann Beach
Mr. Waldo	Ray Smith
Sinbad Sailors	Michael Forrest
Mr. Cherry Owen	Glynn Edwards
Mr. Pugh	Talfryn Thomas
Mr. Willy Nilly	Tim Wylton
Mrs. Willy Nilly	Bronwen Williams
The Rev. Eli Jenkins	Aubrey Richards
Butcher Beynon	Hubert Rees
Mrs. Beynon	Mary Jones
Dai Bread	Dudley Jones
Mrs. Dai Bread One	Dorothea Phillips
Mrs. Dai Bread Two	Ruth Madoc
Organ Morgan	Richard Parry
Mrs. Organ Morgan	Dilys Price
Mae Rose Cottage	Susan Penhaligon
Lily Smalls	Meg Wynn
Utah Watkins	Owen David
Mrs. Utah Watkins	Davies Maudie
Mr. Ogmore	Edwards Dillwyn
Mr. Pritchard	Owen Richard Davies
Lord Cut Glass	Davydd Havard
Norma Jane	Pat Kavanagh

with : Mark Jones, John Rees, Rachel Thomas, Bryn Williams, Paul Grist, Peggy Ann Clifford, Bridget Turner, Davyd Harries, Olwen Rees, Griffith Davies, Andree Gaydon, Shane Shelton, Bryn Jones, John Rainer, Olwen Griffiths,, Paul Spear, Lucy Griffiths, Nesta Harris, Pamela Miles, Janet Davies, Margaret Courtenay, Gwyneth Owen, Gordon Styles, Brian Osborne, T. H. Evans, Edmond Thomas, Jill Britton, Minnie Collins, Rhoda Lewis, Eira Griffiths, Margaret Lace, Angela Brinkworth and Ienan Rhys Williams.

UNDER MILK WOOD

The credits are played over tracking shots beneath a dark night wood. We come closer and closer to the crooked branches of the trees until they almost seem to be seaweed with the reflection of a pale moon beyond.

Dissolve to two seals swimming through a night sea. The first seal goes under a breaker, which rolls over the second seal.

Dissolve to the harbour of Llaregyb, a small fishing-town in Wales. Across on the far quayside, lights shine and blink. Their reflections are swords on the mild whispering black water.

The Two Voices come walking forward beneath the light of a lamp. They wear khaki coats from the Second World War. The First Voice, powerful and brooding, looks back towards the Second Voice, slight and watchful, a jester to the First Voice's Lucifer. We hear his inner thoughts; his lips do not move.

FIRST VOICE : *To begin at the beginning. . .*

Both men move forwards past camera.

We move slowly down from the chapel and roof of the old fishing-town, set on the steep hill-side. We end on a fishing - boat at its moorings in the small port, then cut to a shot of several boats moving on the dark water.

FIRST VOICE : *It is spring, moonless night in the small town, starless and bible-black, the cobble-streets silent and the hunched, courters'-and-rabbits' wood limping invisible down to the sloe-black, slow, black, crowblack, fishing boat-bobbing sea.*

Seen from below, an old Welsh house stands darkly in the powder-black night.

FIRST VOICE : *The houses are blind as moles (though moles see fine tonight in the snouting, velvet dingles) . . .*

At his window, old Captain Cat sits, his milky-blue blind eyes wide open, awake or asleep, for nobody can tell.

FIRST VOICE: *. . . Or blind as Captain Cat, there in the muffled middle . . .*

Pan off Captain Cat and down and cut to a panning shot, seen from above, of the town pump and the town square and the shops, which have their blinds up in their windows, and the houses down the street.

FIRST VOICE : . . . *By the pump and the town clock, the shops in mourning, the Welfare Hall in widows' weeds. And all the people of the lulled and dumbfound town are sleeping now.*

The Two Voices are now walking along the quayside, lifting their feet exaggeratedly high and putting them down very softly, with all the excessive caution of tipsy people. They pass the undertaker's shop, and then the policeman's house with its blue lamp.

FIRST VOICE : *Hush, the babies are sleeping, the farmers, the fishers, the tradesmen and pensioners, cobbler, schoolteacher, postman and publican, the undertaker, and the fancy woman, drunkard, dressmaker, preacher, policeman. . .*

Track with them as they walk, and pan to. . . .

The night shallows, where the Dewi River meets the sea in the harbour and two old women bend and rake cockles like two Fates.

FIRST VOICE: . . . *The webfoot cockle women. . .*

Continue the pan on to Mrs. Pugh as she sleeps in her single bed, mouth closed, hands clasped tidily on the sheet, her nose wrinkling in disapproval, absolutely ready for the Day of judgement tomorrow. By her bed, a portrait of a moustached husband.

FIRST VOICE: . . . *And the tidy wives.*

The pan continues along the beautiful lying body of Gossamer Beynon, the butcher's daughter and the town beauty, as she mutters and stretches in her sleep, naked under her white sheet. She sits up in her dream and a veil blows out behind her.

FIRST VOICE : *Young girls lie bedded soft or glide in their dreams, with rings and trousseaux, bridesmaided by glow-worms down the aisles of the organ playing wood.*

In another small bedroom, a small boy tosses under his crumpled sheets, fighting adventures in his sleep.

FIRST VOICE : *The boys are dreaming wicked or of the bucking ranches of the night and the jollyrodgered sea . . .*

12

Against the sky and the stars, the coaly shapes of two horses.
Silence.

FIRST VOICE : . . . *And the anthracite statues of the horses sleep in the fields. . .*

In a byre, a contented cow licks at the grubby and fat and ugly cowgirl, Bessie Bighead.

FIRST VOICE : . . . *And the cows in the byres. . .*

There is the sound of a dog howling. Bessie moves in her sleep.

FIRST VOICE : . . . *And the dogs in the wetnosed yards.*

Along the ridge of a white-dark roof, two ginger cats glide about their business. We move with them.

FIRST VOICE : . . . *And the cats nap in the slant corners or lope sly, streaking and needling, on the one cloud of the roofs.*

Now the First Voice looks at us urgently in medium close-up.

FIRST VOICE : *You can hear the dew falling, and the hushed town breathing.*

We move off him, and cut to . . .

The edge of the roof, where one ginger cat leaps to the ground, and we move after it as it streaks away.

FIRST VOICE : *Only* your *eyes are unclosed to see the black and folded town fast. . .*

Now Captain Cat is seen from behind, smoking a cheroot, watching the dark sea.

FIRST VOICE : . . . *And slow, asleep. And you alone can hear the invisible starfall, the darkest-before-dawn minutely dewgrazed stir of the black, dab-filled sea. . .*

In the harbour, the fishing-boats slap and rock.

FIRST VOICE : . . . *Where the* Arethusa, *the* Curlew *and the* Skylark, Zanzibar, Rhiannon, *the* Rover, *the* Cormorant, *and the* Star of Wales *tilt and ride.*

Now the First Voice holds up his finger to his mouth, counselling silence to his friend on tiptoes in the silent town. They are elaborately quiet, as they make their way down Cockle Row from where it meets Coronation Street, below Captain Cat's Schooner House.

FIRST VOICE : *Listen. It is night moving in the streets, the processional salt slow musical wind in Coronation Street and Cockle Row. . .*

Above the dark wood which fingers down on the belled steeple of a church, the moon shines fitfully between clouds.

FIRST VOICE : *It is the grass growing on Llaregyb Hill, dewfall, starfall, the sleep of birds in Milk Wood. Listen. It is night in the chill, squat chapel. . .*

We move and pan across the aisle of the chapel between dark pews towards the open bible on the minister's place on high. There is the sound of rustling stiff cloth, coughing, murmuring - but no people are there.

FIRST VOICE : . . . *Hymning in bonnet and brooch and bombazine black, butterfly choker and bootlace bow, coughing like nannygoats, sucking mintoes, fortywinking hallelujah. . .*

In the Sailor's Arms, we continue the movement across the empty pews of the pub drinkers, to end on the twin brass gleaming handles of the beer pumps.

FIRST VOICE : . . . *Night in the four-ale, quiet as a domino*

Now we are inside a bakery, moving over a wooden slab covered with dough and rollers, where Dai Bread the Baker lies asleep, to end on a cold oven full of loaves.

FIRST VOICE : . . . *In Dai Bread's bakery flying like black flour. . .*

Now we are in a loft, moving past a row of empty milk churns, dully pewtered.

14

FIRST VOICE : *In Ocky Milkman's lofts like a mouse with gloves. . . .*

In front of the quayside cottages, the two men fool about. The Second Voice stretches up and catches the cross-bar of the lamp-post under the light and hangs by his hands briefly from the bar, while the First Voice staggers off, no longer carrying his friend on his shoulders.

FIRST VOICE : *It is tonight in Donkey Street, trotting silent, with seaweed on its hooves, along the cockled cobbles, past curtained fern pot, text and trinket, harmonium, holy dresser, watercolours done by hand, china dog and rosy tin teacaddy. It is night neddying among the snuggeries of babies.*

The Second Voice falls down from the lamp-post with a crash. A baby begins to cry. The laughing First Voice picks up his mate.

FIRST VOICE : *Look.*

We cut on their movement to a pan across the overgrown graveyard of the chapel, where brambles spike and crown the tombs.

FIRST VOICE : *It is night, dumbly, royally winding through the Coronation cherry trees, going through the graveyard of Bethesda with winds gloved and folded, and dew doffed. . .*

The sound of a small wind gives way to the sound of creaking, and a pub sign shows a tattooed sailor - his tattoos are the signs of the zodiac. Behind him, the stars and an old galleon. The sign moves in the wind.

FIRST VOICE : *. . . . Tumbling by the Sailor's Arms.*

Now the First Voice is seen in close-up, looking directly into camera, as his inner thoughts speak to us.

FIRST VOICE : *Time passes. Listen. Time passes.*

We move closer in on his piercing eyes.

FIRST VOICE : *Come closer now. Only you can hear the houses sleeping in the streets in the slow deep salt and silent black, bandaged night.*

Now we are in a bedroom, slowly panning from the tidy window-lace over the make-up articles at the dressing table. In its mirror, we see the neat Myfanwy Price asleep in her white wool bed-jacket,. embroidered with red hearts.

FIRST VOICE : *Only you can see, in the blinded bedrooms, the corns. and petticoats over the chairs, the jugs and basins. . .*

Now we continue the movement in another bedroom, starting on a white jug and basin. In the middle of the basin, a pair of shiny black boots. Move onto a glass with false teeth in it, then on past an old family photograph of twenty stiff black Welshmen and Welshwomen in their Sunday best, then on to a skull lying on a pillow, wearing a black woman's hat above and a black dress below. By the side of the skull sleeps the fat barber and herbalist, gentle Mr. Waldo, his plump pink hands, palms up, over the edge of the patchwork quilt. His bowler hangs on a nail above the bed, while a comforter embroidered with THE WAGES OF SIN IS DEATH hangs on the wall above the skull.

FIRST VOICE : *. . . The glasses of teeth, Thou Shalt Not on the wall, and the yellowing dickybird-watching pictures of the dead. Only you can hear and see, behind the eyes of the sleepers, the movements and countries and mazes and colours and dismays and rainbows and tunes and wishes and flight and fall and despairs and big seas of their dreams.*

Now we see the hypnotic eyes of the First Voice as they fill the screen.

FIRST VOICE : *From where you are, you can hear their dreams.*
We cut suddenly to the milky-blue blind eyes of Captain Cat, as he lies in his bunk, then we pull back in a see-saw motion like the sea. Breakers sound, and distant sailors' songs and voices.

FIRST VOICE : *Captain Cat, the retired blind sea captain, asleep in his bunk in the seashelled, ship-in-bottled, shipshape best cabin of Schooner House dreams of . . .*
The rocking movement now seems to make a ship's model near the blind sea-Captain's bed rock in air.

SECOND VOICE : *Never such seas as any that swamped the decks of his S.S.* Kidwelly *bellying over the bedclothes and jellyfishslippery .. .*
The face of the Second Voice is suddenly seen in close-up, hanging upside-down.

SECOND VOICE : *. . . Sucking him down salt deep into the Davy dark where the fish come biting out . . .*
Now the face of the First Voice is seen topsy-turvy and laughing. Now we pull back from the Second Voice to show him hanging by the back of his knees to a cross-piece on the mast of a fishing-boat moored to the quay. As we watch, he falls down onto a pile of mackerel below him. The First Voice watches from the boat, laughing, as the Second Voice pretends to eat a dead fish.

SECOND VOICE : *. . . And nibble him down to his wishbone. . .*
The sound of the breakers now becomes actual rollers, with seals' heads riding the waves.

SECOND VOICE : *. . . And the long drowned nuzzle up to him.*
A pale sailor's face swims up from the dark to declare itself.

FIRST DROWNED'S VOICE : *Remember me, Captain?*
Captain Cat lies in his bunk, lost in his vision of the sea.

CAPTAIN CAT : *You're Dancing Williams!*
The first sailor looms up from the dark and is gone.

FIRST DROWNED'S VOICE : *I lost my step in Nantucket.*
Now another sailor's face swims up from the dark.

SECOND DROWNED'S VOICE : *Do you see me, Captain? The white bone talking? I'm Tom-Fred the donkeyman . . . we shared the same girl once . . . her name was Mrs. Probert . . .*

17

As the face disappears, we are moving into the violet eyes of a beautiful woman sitting on a Welsh brass bed. The edge of the frame is grey with the gauze of memory.

ROSIE PROBERT'S VOICE : *Rosie Probert, thirty-three Duck Lane. Come on up, boys, I'm dead.*

A bearded man's face now swims up from the dark.

THIRD DROWNED'S VOICE : *Hold me, Captain, I'm Jonah Jarvis, come to a bad end, very enjoyable.*

A face, dripping with water and sharp-nosed on fat shoulders tattooed with mermaids, swims forward. It laughs drunkenly.

FOURTH DROWNED'S VOICE : *Alfred Pomeroy Jones, sea-lawyer, born in Mumbles, sung like a linnet, crowned you with a flagon, tattood with mermaids, thirst like a dredger, died of blisters.*

Another bearded face of a handsome sailor now swims forward through waves of darkness.

FIRST DROWNED'S VOICE : *The skull at your earhole is ... .*

FIFTH DROWNED'S VOICE : *Curly Bevan. Tell my auntie it was me that pawned the ormulu clock.*

Captain Cat smiles on his pillow.

CAPTAIN CAT : *Aye, aye, Curly.*

Backed by darkness, the five drowned sailors stand at a bar, talking towards camera, ignoring their drinks.

SECOND DROWNED'S VOICE : *Tell my missus no I never.*

THIRD DROWNED'S VOICE : *I never done what she said I never.*

FOURTH DROWNED'S VOICE : *Yes they did.*

Lights now go up to show the sailors are standing in a smoky pub, as the camera moves in on the face of the First Drowned Sailor.

FIFTH DROWNED : *And who brings coconuts and shawls and parrots to my Gwen now?*

FIRST DROWNED : *How's it above?*

As the sailors talk, the camera rocks and moves back and forth over their speaking faces like the sea-waves.

SECOND DROWNED : *Is there rum and laverbread?*

THIRD DROWNED : *Bosoms and robins?*

FOURTH DROWNED : *Concertinas?*

FIFTH DROWNED : *Ebenezer's bell?*

FOURTH DROWNED : *Fighting and onions?*

THIRD DROWNED : *And sparrows and daisies?*

SECOND DROWNED : *Tiddlers in a jam jar?*

FIRST DROWNED : *Buttermilk and whippets?*

SECOND DROWNED : *Rock-a-bye baby?*

THIRD DROWNED : *Washing on the line?*

FOURTH DROWNED : *And old girls in the snug?*

FIFTH DROWNED : *How's the tenors in Dowlais?*

FOURTH DROWNED : *Who milks the cows in Maesgwyn?*

THIRD DROWNED : *When she smiles, is there dimples?*

FOURTH DROWNED : *What's the smell of parsley?*

> The Fifth Drowned Sailor now starts to sing the old sad Welsh sea-shanty 'Santiana'. As he sings, we dissolve backwards and forwards between Captain Cat, tears now reddening his blind eyes, and the singer and the other sailors, listening. The song ends, and we dissolve back to the old weeping sea-Captain, as he starts up in his bunk.

CAPTAIN CAT : *Oh, my dead dears!*

> We cut on a quick tilt down to where the First Voice stands looking up at Schooner House. Behind him, the Second Voice approaches, gives him a whisky-bottle, and takes him off down the night quayside street.

FIRST VOICE : *From where you are you can hear in Cockle Row in the spring, moonless night, Miss Price, dressmaker and sweet-shop keeper, dream of . . .*

> Now we see the contented, smiling, dreaming, sweet face of Myfanwy Price. She wears a little knitted bedjacket patterned with hearts and lies neat and tidy in her unwrinkled bed.

SECOND VOICE : *. . . Her lover, tall as the town clock tower, Samson-syrup-gold maned, whacking thighed and piping hot. . .*

> Inside Mog Edwards' emporium, yellow and orange curtains hide the approaching figure of her lover. Wearing a blue-suit and a straw hat, he strides on, poses, and strides off.

SECOND VOICE : *. . . Thunderbolt-bass'd and barnacle-breasted, flailing up the cockles with his eyes like blowlamps . . .*

> Myfanwy Price is suddenly hot and writhing in a red night dress with pearls round her neck, as a black figure bends and embraces her.

SECOND VOICE : ... *And scooping low over her lonely loving hotwaterbottled body.*

MOG EDWARDS : *Myfanwy Price!*

MYFANWY PRICE : *Mr. Mog Edwards!*

Start on the blaze of bright materials through which the shape of Myfanwy's lover advanced. The materials are still swinging. Then pan and move towards Mog Edwards standing behind the ornamented till on the counter of his shop. He is backed by bolts of cloth of dull colours, and fronted by cases of buttons and needles and thread. All over the shop run little wires for sending accounts in directions that end in himself. As he speaks, he automatically writes a bill, puts the bill and a pound note into the container on the wire, pushes it off along the wires, receives it back again, takes out the bill and money, rings up a sale, opens the till, converts the money into change, stamps the receipt, wraps up the change in the receipt, replaces it in the container, and sends it back to himself. Containers keep on arriving and leaving him, while he madly rings up sales faster and faster, taking and making money by himself.

MOG EDWARDS : *I am a draper mad with love. I love you more than all the flannelette and calico, candlewick, dimity, crash and merino, tussore, cretonne, crepon, muslin, poplin, ticking and twill in the whole Cloth Hall of the world. I have come to take you away to my emporium on the hill. Throw away your little bedsocks and your Welsh wool knitted jacket, I will warm the sheets like an electric toaster, I will lie by your side like the Sunday roast.*

Myfanwy Price is still writhing on the red sheets of her dreams, biting her pearls.

MYFANWY PRICE : *I will knit you a wallet of forget-me-not blue, for the money to be comfy. I will warm your heart by the fire so that you can slip it in under your vest when the shop is closed.*

Mog Edwards is still madly sending and receiving containers on his wires, and ringing his till.

MOG EDWARDS : *Myfanwy, Myfanwy, before the mice gnaw at your bottom drawer, will you say . . . ?*

Myfanwy is in ecstasy of dream delight.

MYFANWY PRICE : *Yes, Mog, yes, Mog, yes, yes, yes.*

Mog Edwards rings up his change madly and works the wires, while church bells also sound.

MOG EDWARDS : *And all the bells of the tills of the town shall ring for our wedding.*

Cut to the First and Second Voices. They seem to be looking for something or someone, as they shrug and slip their way up the street. The camera moves with them in the slow rocking of a ship's deck.

FIRST VOICE : *Come now, drift up the dark, come up the drifting sea-dark street now in the dark night seesawing like the sea . . .*

On the same line of motion, we are coming up to the window of an attic bedroom, and are suddenly inside the room, coming up on a stern dark man, Jack Black the Cobbler, putting on his elastic bands that keep his nightshirt down, knotting his whip-belt round his waist, and picking up his Bible as he goes out into the satanic night.

FIRST VOICE :. . . *To the bible-black airless attic over Jack Black the cobbler's shop.*

JACK BLACK : *Ach y fi! Ach y fi!*

Over the fork of a yew tree in a churchyard, Jack Black appears, his whip-belt ready. He descends on a loving couple, later found to be Nogood Boyo and Mae Rose Cottage. She screams and runs.

JACK BLACK : *Ach y fi! Ach y fi!*

He chases Nogood away through the gravestones.

Now in a bar, the drunken Nogood Boyo does not see Jack Black enter, howling with his whip.

JACK BLACK : *Ach y fi! Ach y fi!*

He flogs Nogood down onto the bar.

There is the sound of organ music, which changes to a dance organ, as we see the well-dressed Nogood Boyo now dancing with Gossamer Beynon, while another man, later identified as P.C. Attila Rees, dances with Mae Rose Cottage.

Again Jack Black appears and whips the men away from the screaming girls.

JACK BLACK : *Ach y fi! Ach y fi! Ach y fi!*

Outside the undertaker's shop on the quayside, the reflections of the First and Second Voices show on the lettered window, as they stand looking in at the tombstones and coffins advertising funerals. Move with the laughing Second Voice to show Evans the Death lying in his bed by the window. He is also laughing and his feet stick out at the end of the bed. He curls his toes through a hole in his sock. A coffin stands open by his side.

SECOND VOICE : *Evans the Death, the undertaker, runs out into the field where his mother is making welshcakes in the snow, and steals a fistful of snowflakes and currants and climbs back into bed to eat them cold and sweet under the warm white clothes. . .*

Now we see Mr. Waldo, the fat man, lying in his bed by the skull.

SECOND VOICE : *While Mr. Waldo, rabbitcatcher, barber, herbalist, catdoctor, quack, dreams of . . .*

Inside an old Welsh kitchen, Waldo's mother rolls dough on a slab. We pan across to show Waldo, now dreamt into a Fat Boy, as he makes two patties out of coal dust and comes up with them on his mother.

WALDO'S MOTHER :

> *This little piggy went to market*
> *This little piggy stayed at home*
> *This little piggy had roast beef*
> *This little piggy had none*
> *And this little piggy went . . .*

FAT BOY WALDO : *Wee wee wee wee wee.*

WALDO'S MOTHER : *All the way home to Waldo's mum . . .*

Fat Boy Waldo plomps the coal-cakes onto his mother's dough, and she rolls them in, before seeing what she has done!

WALDO'S MOTHER : *Waldo!*

She pursues her son into the farmyard with her rolling-pin. Now back to the bedroom where the fat pink Waldo still lies sleeping with his wife's skull in her black hat on the pillow beside him. Tears run from the skull's sockets.

SKULL : *Waldo! Wal-do!*

MR. WALDO : muttering in his sleep : *Yes, Blodwen love?*

SKULL :. . .Oh, *Waldo!*

MR. WALDO : *Hush, love, hush. I'm* widower *Waldo now.*

SKULL : *Oh, what'll the neighbours say, what'll the neighbours . .*

Two fierce Neighbour women now talk to each other by a flowering garden wall.

THIRD NEIGHBOUR : *Black as a chimbley . . .*

FOURTH NEIGHBOUR : *Ringing doorbells . . .*

THIRD NEIGHBOUR : *Breaking windows . . .*

FOURTH NEIGHBOUR : *Making mudpies . . .*

THIRD NEIGHBOUR : *Stealing currants . . .*

FOURTH NEIGHBOUR : *Chalking words . . .*

THIRD NEIGHBOUR : *Saw him in the bushes . . .*

FOURTH NEIGHBOUR : *Playing mwchins . . .*

At the back of the wall, unseen by the gossipping neighbours, the Fat Boy Waldo approaches, carrying a dripping mud pie in each hand.

THIRD NEIGHBOUR : *Send him to bed without any supper . . .*

FOURTH NEIGHBOUR : *Give him senna pods and lock him in the dark. . .*

THIRD NEIGHBOUR : *Off to the reformatory . . .*

FOURTH NEIGHBOUR : *Off to the reformatory . . .*

The Fat Boy Waldo drops a mud pie onto each of the gossips' heads and scampers off, while they claw at their hair and scream with rage.

THIRD AND FOURTH NEIGHBOURS : *Learn him with a slipper on his b.t.m.*

While they try to get the mud from their hair, another mother screams after the Fat Boy Waldo, as a dog outbarks her.

MOTHER'S VOICE : *Waldo, Wal-do! What you doing with our Matti?*

Under a bridge by a stream, the Fat Boy Waldo and a little girl crouch. They fondle each other, but the girl backs from the boy's kiss.

FAT BOY WALDO : *Give us a kiss, Matti Richards.*

LITTLE GIRL : *Give us a penny then.*

FAT BOY WALDO : *Norma Jane's a halfpenny.*

LITTLE GIRL : *Silly old her.*

Now the adult Mr. Waldo is seen, as he wears his bowler hat and brown suit and looks very unhappy. An organ sounds.

MR. WALDO : *I only got a halfpenny.*

Move back to show a young woman by his side. She wears a wedding-veil and obviously stands by him in a chapel.

FIRST WIFE : *Lips is a penny.*

> Seen from below, the Reverend Eli Jenkins leans forward in his pulpit. He is a wise, loving, luminous, slightly ridiculous, Welsh preacher, with long white Bardic hair.

REVEREND ELI JENKINS : *Will you take this woman, Matti Richards . . . ?*

> We slowly move out from Waldo by his First Wife to show him by Five other Wives and a skeleton, all in wedding dresses. He looks appalled.
>
> The Reverend Jenkins looks down on all of them from his pulpit.

SECOND WIFE : *Dulcie Prothero.*

THIRD WIFE : *Effie Bevan.*

FOURTH WIFE : *Lil the Gluepot.*

FIFTH WIFE : *Mrs. Flusher.*

> We cut back to the stern foolish Reverend.

REVEREND ELI JENKINS : . . . *To be your awful wedded wife?*

> Now back to Waldo's face, as he opens his mouth in a scream, backed by organ chords.

MR. WALDO : *No, no, no!*

Now the First Voice, devilish and laughing soundlessly, turns on the quayside to see . . .

The Second Voice as he pantomimes cleaning and scrubbing with a handkerchief outside *Bay View,* one of a line of villas, built in the 1930's and rather out-of-keeping with the rest of the old Welsh town.

FIRST VOICE : *Now, in her iceberg-white, holily laundered crinoline nightgown, under virtuous polar sheets, in her spruced and scoured dust-defying bedroom in trig and trim Bay View, a house for paying guests, at the top of the town, Mrs. Ogmore-Pritchard widow, twice, of Mr. Ogmore, linoleum, retired, and Mr. Pritchard, failed bookmaker, who maddened by the voice of the vacuum-cleaner and the fume of polish, ironically swallowed disinfectant . . .*

Move from the two men now up towards the dark blinded bedroom window of *Bay View . . .*

Then move up from a polished floor over a bedpost to show Mrs. Ogmore-Pritchard, a terrifying and steely Welsh lady, as she lies in her big bed between Mr. Ogmore and Mr. Pritchard, both pale and obedient. She is in nightgown and cap, they in pyjamas.

FIRST VOICE : *. . . Fidgets in her rinsed sleep, wakes in a dream, and nudges in the ribs dead Mr. Ogmore, dead Mr. Pritchard, ghostly on either side.*

MRS. OGMORE-PRITCHARD : *Mr. Ogmore! Mr. Pritchard! It is time to inhale your balsam.*

MR. OGMORE : *Oh, Mrs. Ogmore!*

MR. PRITCHARD : *Oh, Mrs. Pritchard!*

MRS. OGMORE-PRITCHARD: *Soon it will be time to get up. Tell me your tasks, in order.*

MR. OGMORE : *I must put my pyjamas in the drawer marked pyjamas.*

MR. PRITCHARD : *I must take my cold bath which is good for me.*

MR.OGMORE : *I must wear my flannel band to ward off sciatica.*

MR. PRITCHARD : *I must dress behind the curtain and put on my apron.*

MR. OGMORE : *I must blow my nose.*

MRS. OGMORE-PRITCHARD : *In the garden, if you please.*

MR. OGMORE : *In a piece of tissue-paper which I afterwards burn.*

MR. PRITCHARD *: I must take my salts which are nature's friend.*

MR. OGMORE : *I must boil the drinking water because of germs.*

MR. PRITCHARD : *I must make my herb tea which is free from tannin.*

MR. OGMORE : *And have a charcoal biscuit which is good for me.*

MR. PRITCHARD : *I may smoke one pipe of asthma mixture.*

MRS. OGMORE-PRITCHARD : *In the woodshed, if you please.*

MR. PRITCHARD : *And dust the parlour and spray the canary.*

MR. OGMORE : *I must put on rubber gloves and search the peke for fleas.*

MR. PRITCHARD : *I must dust the blinds and then I must raise them.*

MRS. OGMORE-PRITCHARD : *And before you let the sun in, mind it wipes its shoes.*

We move in onto Mrs. Ogmore-Pritchard's disapproving expression as she speaks, then we cut to . . . Gossamer Beynon's bedroom, where Gossamer dreams fiercely, blowing feathers from her ripped pillow.

FIRST VOICE : *In Butcher Beynon's, Gossamer Beynon, daughter, schoolteacher, dreaming deep . . .*

Now we cut to the Sailor's Arms, where the black-bearded and melancholy Sinbad Sailors fiercely pulls at his beer-pumps.

SECOND VOICE : *Sinbad Sailors in the Sailor's Arms pulls the pumps whose secret name is . . .*

SINBAD SAILORS : *Gossamer . . . Gossamer .. .*

Now Sinbad is pulling Gossamer's ankles like beer pumps as she lies laughing and belly-down on her bed.

SINBAD SAILORS : *Gossamer . . . Gossamer . . .*

Now we cut to the bedroom of P.C. Attila Rees, as he slowly gets out of bed, picks up his helmet, and sits upon it like a pot.

SECOND VOICE : *P.C. Attila Rees lumps out of bed, dead to the dark and deep in the backyard lockup of his sleep . . . You'll be sorry for that in the morning.*

26

The dream sequences and night part of the picture end, as we go to . . .

A hilltop by the Druid circle of ancient stones, overlooking the dawn sea and the harbour and the town. There the First Voice stands alone. The dream music fades. There is silence.

FIRST VOICE : *Time passes. Listen. Time passes. An owl flies home past Bethesda, to a chapel in an oak. And the dawn inches up.*

We pan along the distant quayside, showing the whole length of Cockle Row with the hills of Wales beyond.

FIRST VOICE : *Stand on this hill. This is Llaregyb Hill. Old as the hills, high, cool, and green, and from this small circle of stones, made by the Druids for a come-to-visit Milk Wood . . .*

As we pan on round the view below and past the Druid stones, the First Voice mysteriously is found standing again on the far side of the stones.

FIRST VOICE : . . . *You can see all the town below you sleeping in the first of the dawn.*

In the distance, we hear the sound of larks and gulls. We are suddenly in the town square in front of a red and blue charabanc, decorated with Union Jacks. We pull back to show its seats filled with Tourists from the world over. All wear glasses or eyeshades, or look through cameras. Nobody looks directly at anything through his own eyes. A voice speaks through a loud-speaker, which booms through the empty square. The voice comes from a Guide in a smart blue blazer.

VOICE OF A GUIDE : *Less than five hundred souls inhabit the three quaint streets and the few narrow by-lanes and scattered farmsteads that constitute this small, decaying watering-place which may, indeed, be called a ' backwater of life ' . . .*

Out of the door of the wooden house that looks like a small schooner, the blind old Captain Cat emerges wearing his sailor's cap and seaboots. He is answering the knock of a small Boy, who leads off the blind man.

Camera moves off behind them to show the bay and Cockle Row.

VOICE OF A GUIDE : . . . *Without disrespect to its natives who possess, to this day, a salty individuality of their own. The main street, Coronation Street, consists, for the most part, of humble, two-storied houses, many of which attempt to achieve some measure of gaiety by prinking themselves out in crude colours and by the liberal use of pinkwash . . .*

From a hill above the town, we see the white roofs and the Dewi River in the early sun.

VOICE OF A GUIDE : . . . *Though there are remaining a few eighteenth-century houses of more pretension, if, on the whole, in a sad state of disrepair.*

Back outside the charabanc, we start on the standing figure of the Guide, talking into a microphone and seen through the yellow glass of the bus windows. Then we track slowly all the way round the bus, to meet the gaze of the Tourists through their glasses and cameras through the windows. No one moves in their seats, no one stirs, as they look blankly outside at nothing very much, with a lot more to see ahead of them that day. One Tourist is asleep, another unwinds the spool of film from the back of her camera.

VOICE OF A GUIDE : *Though there is little to attract the hill climber, the healthseeker, the sportsman, or the week-ending motorist, the contemplative may, if sufficiently attracted to spare it some leisurely hours, find, in its cobbled streets and its little*

fishing harbour, in its several curious customs, and in the conver-
sation of its local 'characters', some of that picturesque sense of
the past so frequently lacking in towns and villages which have
kept more abreast of the times.

By the bridge that crosses the Dewi River, Ocky Milkman
stands in the water, scooping it up in a bucket and adding it to
his milk churns on the back of his horse-drawn cart.

VOICE OF A GUIDE : *The River Dewi is said to abound in trout,*
but is much poached.

Beyond a row of ancient graves in the overgrown graveyard,
Captain Cat is led by the boy up the hill from the bay through
trees.

VOICE OF A GUIDE : *The one place of worship, with its*
neglected graveyard, is of no architectural interest.

The bus now throws up a cloud of dust as it snorts away, a red
Welsh dragon painted on its rear. As it leaves, Ocky Milkman
rounds the corner of the square, leading his horse and milk-
cart.

From the top of the hill overlooking the town, the First Voice
begins to walk down to where the Second Voice waits for his
friend, looking at his watch as though they had some
appointment. Both begin to move back towards the town.

FIRST VOICE : *The principality of the sky lightens now, over our*
green hill, into spring morning larked and crowed and belling.

A faint bell-note sounds as the camera moves onto Milk
Wood above the houses.

Inside the chapel; Captain Cat pulls on the bell-rope, rising
off the ground with every swing of the bell. From the
chimneys of the town, the first puffs of smoke come out like
slow upflying snow.

Now we see the chapel bell swinging in the little peaked
steeple of the chapel.

Bethesda House, where the Reverend Eli Jenkins lives by his
chapel, is built in the Welsh Georgian style, white with fan
windows, on the hill overlooking the sea. To the sound of the
sea breaking and the gab of the birds between the notes of the
bell ringing, the Reverend Eli Jenkins comes out of his front
door. His black preacher's suit is in disarray about him, he is

unshaven, but a look of radiance and peace crosses his face as he salutes the morning.

ELI JENKINS :

> *Dear Gwalia! I know there are*
> *Towns lovelier than ours*
> *And fairer hills and loftier far . . .*

Cut to flowering white trees against the steep slope of a wooded hill.

ELI JENKINS VOICE :

> *And groves more full of flowers*
> *And boskier woods more blithe with spring . . .*

Now cut to a picture-postcard view of a Welsh valley nestling under hills and budding woods with birdsong loud around.

ELI JENKINS VOICE :

> *. . . And bright with birds' adorning*
> *And sweeter bards than I to sing . . .*

Now we are back on a medium close-up of the Reverend Jenkins in front of Bethesda House.

ELI JENKINS :

> *Their praise this beauteous morning . . .*

We pan across a valley, where a white farmhouse lies below a dark mountain . . .

ELI JENKINS VOICE :

> *By mountains where King Arthur dreams*
> *By Penmaenmawr defiant . . .*

Now we are close on the Reverend Jenkins.

> *. . . Llaregyb Hill a molehill seems*
> *A pygmy to a giant.*

Now we pan down a Welsh river as it races over a rocky waterfall.

ELI JENKINS VOICE :

> *By Sawdde, Senny, Dulais, Daw,*
> *Ely, Gwili, Ogwr, Nedd . . .*

The First Voice looks up at camera, standing by a little brown stream. He walks off followed by the Second Voice.

ELI JENKINS VOICE :

> *. . . Small is our River Dewi, Lord,*
> *A baby on a rushy bed.*

Seen from underneath, the mighty ruin of Carreg Cennen Castle towers on its rock.

ELI JENKINS VOICE :

> *By Carreg Cennen, King of time . . .*

Seen from above, we see a headland sticking out into the dawn sea. Gulls wheel about.

ELI JENKINS VOICE :

> *Our Heron Head is only . . .*

Now we see the dawn sun beyond the headland and the gulls that float in air.

ELI JENKINS VOICE :

> *. . . A bit of stone with seaweed spread . . .*

The light of the new sun shines on the Reverend's face.

ELI JENKINS :

> *. . . Where gulls come to be lonely.*
> *A tiny dingle is Milk Wood . . .*

Now we see Captain Cat led by the boy returning home from under Milk Wood, across the Dewi bridge. Pan with them to show the whole harbour and quayside, bright with the new day's sun.

ELI JENKINS VOICE :

> *. . . By Golden Grove 'neath Grongar,*
> *But let me choose and oh! I should*
> *Love all my life and longer*
> *To stroll among our trees and stray*
> *In Goosegog Lane, on Donkey Down,*
> *And hear the Dewi sing all day . . .*

There is yearning and conviction in the Reverend's face, as he finishes his little poem.

ELI JENKINS :

> *. . . And never, never leave the town.*

He walks back towards Bethesda House, then stops and turns back for a last comment.

ELI JENKINS : *Morning Service is over. Thank you, God bach, for listening. Who else would?*

Inside the tiled murder of Butcher Beynon's shop, Lily Smalls, Mrs. Beynon's treasure, rubs her eyes. She is yawning, but she smiles to see the picture of the Queen on the cover of the magazine on the pile of paper the butcher uses to wrap the chops in.

LILY SMALLS : *There's a lady!*

MRS. BEYNON'S VOICE : *Lily!*

LILY SMALLS : *And there isn't!*

She drags off.

Now Lily Smalls comes into the kitchen and wearily puts the kettle on the stove. She tidies from the night before in the dirtiest way possible. A great black cat mews at her heels. She gives it beer in a saucer, but keeps on returning to admire her reflection in a shaving-mirror and a handmirror, while she makes the tea.

LILY SMALLS : *Oh there's a face!*

Where you get that hair from?

Got it from an old tom cat.

Give it back then, love.

Oh there's a perm!

Where you get that nose from, Lily?

Got it from my father, silly.

You've got it on upside down!

Oh there's a conk!

Look at your complexion!

Oh no, you look.

Needs a bit of make-up.

Needs a veil.

Oh there's glamour!

Where you get that smile, Lil?

Never you mind, girl.

Nobody loves you.

That's what you think.

Who is it loves you?

Shan't tell.

Come on, Lily.

Cross your heart then?

Cross my heart.

32

She leans forward so that her lips are almost touching the shaving-glass, then she breathes the name of her lover and clouds the glass.

LILY SMALLS : *The Prince of Wales . . .*

MRS. BEYNON'S VOICE : *Lily!*

LILY SMALLS : *Yes, mum.*

MRS. BEYNON'S VOICE : *Where's my tea, girl?*

LILY SMALLS : *Where d'you think?*

She dumps the steaming tea-pot in the middle of the cat-box. The great black cat turns its green eyes up to the heavens.

LILY SMALLS : *Coming up, mum.*

On a staircase in the Pugh household, we start on another pot of tea and a full cup and a biscuit in a saucer on the tray held in Mr. Pugh's hand as he slowly walks up the stairs. Move with him as he goes across the landing to the door of his wife's bedroom. He looks small and sinister, another Crippen with his drooping moustache.

MR. PUGH *to himself* :

> *Here's your arsenic, dear.*
> *And your weedkiller biscuit.*
> *I've throttled your parakeet.*
> *I've spat in the vases.*
> *I've put cheese in the mouseholes.*
> *Here's your . . .*

He opens the bedroom door and enters.. . .

The bedroom, where his expression changes to one of brown sugar sweetness as he approaches his wife's bed with the tray.

MR. PUGH :. . . *Nice tea, dear.*

Mrs. Pugh sits up, night-gowned and fierce.

MRS. PUGH : *Too much sugar.*

MR. PUGH : *You haven't tasted it yet, dear.*

MRS. PUGH : *Too much milk, then. Has Mr. Jenkins said his poetry?*

MR. PUGH : *Yes, dear.*

MRS. PUGH : *Then it's time to get up. Give me my glasses.*

Mr. Pugh takes up the wrong pair of glasses from their case by the bed.

MRS. PUGH : *No, not my reading glasses, I want to look out.*

Mr. Pugh gives her the other pair of glasses from its identical case, as Mrs. Pugh perches the glasses on her nose and leans forwards to peer out of the window into the street.

MRS. PUGH : *I want to see!*

Seen from Mrs. Pugh's point of view, Lily Smalls sloshes and scrubs at the steps of the butcher's shop, her dress tucked into her bloomers. Mrs. Pugh is steely with indignation to her husband at her window.

MRS. PUGH : *Oh, the baggage!*

She peers out again in a different direction, this time leaning over the windowsill to see further down the street. Seen from above by Mrs. Pugh, P.C. Attila Rees mops his damp helmet with his handkerchief, as, ox-broad and bargebooted, he stamps out of Handcuff House in a heavy beefred huff. His nose wrinkles with distaste as he smells the interior of his helmet before putting it on unwillingly over his black eye-brows.

At her window, Mrs. Pugh comments to her husband, who is rolling up a napkin in the background.

MRS. PUGH : *He's going to arrest Polly Garter, mark my words.*

Now we are on the quayside, where Polly Garter, the town's easy woman, walks along smiling past the ladies' disapproval, followed by the happy P.C. Rees.

MR. PUGH'S VOICE : *What for, dear?*

Back at the window, Mrs. Pugh's mouth clamps with dis-approval.

MRS. PUGH : *For having babies.*

She cranes her head out even further to have a look. Inside the room, Mr. Pugh rolls up his napkin into a rope.

MR. PUGH : *Perhaps he's going to the dock to see that the sea is still there.*

Mrs. Pugh looks up into the light and the first floor windows. Above the Sailor's Arms, Sinbad's grandmother, the radiant Mary Ann Sailors, calls out to the heavens from her window.

MARY ANN SAILORS : *I'm eighty-five years, three months and a day!*

Choirs of children's voices back her faith.

At her own window, Mrs. Pugh comments inescapably.

MRS. PUGH : *I will say this for her, she never makes a mistake.*

She sees something in the street and her brows knit together. Ominous music sounds.

Seen from above in a long shot, then a closer shot, the First and the Second Voices come sauntering down the street, looking at the windows for something, some one . . . Mrs. Pugh is disturbed at her window, with her husband small and little in the background, winding the napkin into a hangman's knot.

MRS. PUGH : *There's strangers. Up to no good.*

MR. PUGH : *Perhaps they're just visitors.*

MRS. PUGH : *If they're just visitors, how don't I know them?*

Mr. Pugh pulls the napkin with his teeth, tightening the noose round his wrist as if it were her neck .

At his windowsill over his wife's general store, Organ Morgan is playing at the organ - and indeed, organ music sounds.

It is suddenly cut short, as gull's droppings hit his face.

Above, the gulls wheel about, heckling like housewives. Organ Morgan sadly withdraws into his bedroom.

Now Dai Bread hurries down the street from his house in the square, half-dressed and muttering to himself. He fiddles with a key at the lock of the bakery.

DAI BREAD : *Me, Dai Bread, hurrying to the bakery, pushing in my shirt-tails, buttoning my waistcoat, ping goes a button, why can't they sew them, no time for breakfast, nothing for breakfast, there's wives for you.*

Outside the Dai Bread house, the fat, capped, shawled and comfy Mrs. Dai Bread One clatters in her clogs down the cobbles to stir up her neighbours on their doorsteps.

Behind, lolling gaudy from the doorway, follows Mrs. Dai Bread Two. She is dressed gypsied to kill in a silky scarlet petticoat above her dirty pretty knees. There are holes in her petticoat showing her body, brown as a berry. She wears high-heeled shoes with one heel missing, and a tortoiseshell comb in her bright black shiny hair. Nothing else she has on but a dab of scent, and she fondles her crystal ball.

MRS. DAI BREAD TWO : *Where are you going, Mrs. Dai Bread One?*

MRS. DAI BREAD ONE : *Just off to borrow a loaf, Mrs. Two. Won't be long.*

She hurries off.

Passing now is Lord Cut-Glass, wearing a pair of postman's trousers and an old frock-coat of the Reverend Eli Jenkins.

He jerks to the beat of the time that only he can hear.

MRS. DAI BREAD TWO : *Tell your fortune in the tea leaves, Lord Cut-Glass?*

LORD CUT-GLASS : *Tick tock tick tock. Must rush, Mrs. Dai Bread.*

Scared, Lord Cut-Glass jerks away.

MRS. DAI BREAD TWO laughing : *Two. Mrs. Dai Bread Two. Not Mrs. One, she's another. Tick tock* two.

Mrs. Dai Bread Two laughs evilly into camera.

In Jack Black the Cobbler's shop, a hand is seen hammering a scarlet shoe. Another angle shows Jack Black at his bench by the fire, fondling the red shoe that must be Mrs. Dai Bread Two's.

JACK BLACK : *There is no leg that belongs to the foot that belongs to this shoe.*

At the doorway of her cottage, Mrs. Sarah sits gingerly on her seat, her little boy by her side, ready to go to school. Mrs. Dai Bread One jollies and jellies in to sit down beside her.

MRS. DAI BREAD ONE : *Oh, Mrs. Sarah, can you spare a loaf, love? Dai Bread forgot the bread.*

She settles in a chair by Mrs. Sarah.

MRS. SARAH : *Of course, you can have a loaf, Mrs. Dai Bread One. Go get a loaf, love.*

She pushes her little boy inside the door to fetch the bread.

MRS. DAI BREAD ONE : *There's a lovely morning! How's your boils this morning?*

MRS. SARAH : *Going down nicely.*

Seen through the window of her living-room on the quayside, Myfanwy Price finishes her breakfast laid out on a little table, an egg in its bright cosy, a tea-pot in its cheery cover, toast-fingers, home-made plum jam in a glass pot and a butterpat made into the shape of a cottage. Miss Price rises and goes out. We move with her across the bright front of her sweetshop, and pan to where two little girls come running up, their school satchels over their shoulders. They rap with pennies in their hands on the glass panel of the sweetshop. Miss Price changes a little placard from CLOSED to OPEN, opens the shop door, takes the children's pennies, and gives them two lollipops.

MYFANWY PRICE : *Good morning . . . There we are, Happy . . .*

The little girls run off to school, while Miss Price turns back into the shop, smoothing her apron.

At his clothing emporium near the square, Mog Edwards opens the shutters over his shop windows, to reveal his little haberdasher's empire of cloth and etceteras. Then he turns in his dandy brown suit and straw hat to measure the dawdlers-by for clothes. In turn, an old man with his dog, a matron, and a girl pass without stopping.

MOG EDWARDS : *You, Mister Criminal, I'll put you behind bars. A striped flannel shirt for only thirty-nine and eleven. For you, madam, a best shroud. For you, a flowery blouse . . . I love Miss Myfanwy Price.*

In her sweetshop that also serves general goods, Myfanwy Price hands a tin of syrup across the counter to a lady shopper.

MYFANWY PRICE : *Three pence off for the rust, but that's outside the tin.*

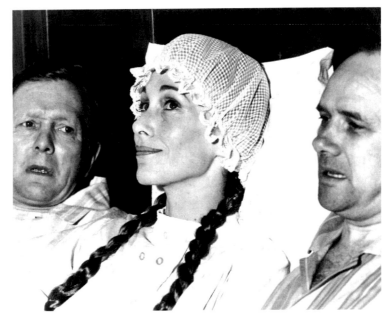

At the back of her tumbledown cottage, Polly Garter throws
mountains of sheets and towels, nearly all the town's washing, over heather and gorse bush. All the time she works with
two hands, a baby lies at her breast, swinging on her stomach
in a shawl tied round her shoulders. Polly is happy and talks
lovingly to her baby.

POLLY GARTER : *Nothing grows in our garden, only washing.
And babies. And where's their fathers live, my love? Over the hills
and far away. Oh, you're looking up at me now. I know what
you're thinking, you poor little milky creature. You're thinking,
you're no better than you should be, Polly Garter, and that's good
enough for me. Oh, isn't life a terrible thing, thank God?*

She looks up and smiles to see gentlemen pass by.

The two Voices walk by Polly's garden, bright with prints
and primroses. They smile to hear the baby's cry..

FIRST VOICE : *Now frying-pans spit, kettles and cats purr in the
kitchen. The town smells of seaweed and breakfast all the way
down from Bay View . . .*

At her dining-table, Mrs. Ogmore-Pritchard in smock and
turban sips at her tea, puts it down, sees a small crumb on the
polished table-top, picks it up, is about to pop it in her mouth,
then puts it away firmly. She then picks up a fly-whisk and

swats at the patch of sunlight on the table, killing a fly by chance.

MRS. OGMORE-PRITCHARD : *Shoo, you old sun. You'll spoil the polish.*

Outside the sunny Sailor's Arms, Sinbad Sailors puts a wooden chair down on the cobbles for his grandmother, who sits down and eats her bowl of porridge.

MARY ANN SAILORS : *Praise the Lord who made porridge.*

In the Pugh kitchen, Mr. Pugh stands by the cooker, juggling an omelette, which he tilts onto a plate. Ominous music sounds, as he sprinkles salt onto the omelette.

MR. PUGH muttering : *Ground glass.*

He takes the omelette through into the dining-room, where Mrs. Pugh sits, nagging at an aspidistra behind the drawn blinds.

MRS. PUGH : *Stand up straight, can't you?*

She puts some of the omelette on her fork, does not eat it, and looks up accusingly at the cringing Mr. Pugh.

As the dream music swells, we cut to a dream sequence where the grinning Mr. Pugh leads the nightgowned Mrs. Pugh off by a rope round her neck. Out of her breast sticks a dagger, while she pulls at the noose round her throat.

SECOND VOICE : *Sly and silent, he foxes into his chemist's den and there, in a hiss and prussic circle of cauldrons and phials brimful with pox and the Black Death, cooks up a fricassee of deadly night-shade, nicotine, hot frog, cyanide and bat-spit.*

Now Mr. Waldo sits up in bed, wearing his bowler and bib, gobbling chips and swigging from a bottle of HP Sauce. He falls asleep again. In Waldo's day-dream, we start on a pile of nasty rubbish, while one Neighbour woman finishes taking down her washing and walks across to join another Neighbour woman, who is fiercely clipping the yellow-green hedge between them.

FIRST NEIGHBOUR : *Poor Mrs. Waldo . . .*

SECOND NEIGHBOUR : *What she puts up with . . .*

FIRST NEIGHBOUR : *Never should have married . . .*

SECOND NEIGHBOUR : *If she didn't had to . . .*

FIRST NEIGHBOUR : *Same as his mother . . .*

SECOND NEIGHBOUR : *There's a husband for you . . .*

FIRST NEIGHBOUR : *Bad as his father . . .*

SECOND NEIGHBOUR : *And you know where he ended.*

FIRST NEIGHBOUR : *Up in the asylum . . .*

SECOND NEIGHBOUR : *Crying for his ma . . .*

FIRST NEIGHBOUR : *Every Saturday . . .*

SECOND NEIGHBOUR : *He hasn't got a leg . . .*

FIRST NEIGHBOUR : *And carrying on . . .*

SECOND NEIGHBOUR : *With that Mrs. Beattie Morris . . .*

FIRST NEIGHBOUR : *Up in the quarry . . .*

SECOND NEIGHBOUR : *And seen her baby . . .*

FIRST NEIGHBOUR : *It's got his nose . . .*

SECOND NEIGHBOUR : *Oh it makes my heart bleed*

FIRST NEIGHBOUR : *What he'll do for drink . . .*

SECOND NEIGHBOUR : *He sold the pianola . . .*

FIRST NEIGHBOUR : *And her sewing machine . . .*

SECOND NEIGHBOUR : *Falling in the gutter . . .*

FIRST NEIGHBOUR : *Talking to the lamp-post .*

SECOND NEIGHBOUR : *Using language . . .*

FIRST NEIGHBOUR : *Singing in the w . . .*

SECOND NEIGHBOUR : *Poor Mrs. Waldo . . .*

Inside his hovel, Lord Cut-Glass sits down to his meal of fish scraps in a dog-dish marked Fido, surrounded by his clocks. He watches them, eats, rises, strokes their faces, and loves them. The kitchen has precious little on its shelves and table except for the clocks, ticking, ticking, ticking. There are sixty-six clocks in all, one for each year of Lord Cut-Glass's age. He jerks in rhythm from one clock to another, winding them, checking on their health.

FIRST VOICE : *Lord Cut-Glass, in his kitchen full of time, listens to the voices of his sixty-six clocks, one for each year of his loony age, and watches, with love, their black-and-white moony loud-lipped faces tocking the earth away : slow clocks, quick clocks, pendulumed heart-knocks, china, alarm, grandfather, cuckoo; clocks shaped like Noah's whirring Ark, clocks that bicker in marble ships, clocks in the wombs of glass women, hourglass chimers, tu-wit-tu-woo clocks, clocks that pluck tunes, Vesuvius clocks all black bells and lava, Niagara clocks that cataract their ticks, old time-weeping clocks with ebony beards, clocks with no hands for ever drumming out time without ever knowing what time it is. His sixty-six singers are all set at different hours. Lord Cut-Glass lives in a house and a life at siege. Any minute or dark day now, the unknown enemy will loot and savage downhill . . .*

Jump cut to a close-up of Lord Cut-Glass as he leaps to his feet in terror, with clock works and hands going mad about him.

FIRST VOICE : *. . . But they will not catch him napping. Sixty-six different times in his fish-slimy kitchen . . .*

Cut to five different close-ups of the works of the clocks, to fit the final words of the speech about Lord Cut-Glass.

FIRST VOICE : *. . . Ping . . . Strike . . . tick . . . chime . . . and tock.*

In the grimy wash-house, the lecherous Nogood Boyo plays on the washboard to the sound of skiffle, and also plays with himself.

NOGOOD BOYO : *Me, Nogood Boyo, up to no good in the wash-house.*

In the comfortable sloppy room of the Cherry Owens on the quayside, Mrs. Cherry Owen brings over a saucepan of broth, while her sleepy husband staggers to the table. There is a real mess of congealed muck on the wallpaper by the photograph of a respectable harridan. Although obviously poor, both the Cherry Owens are merry and loving.

MRS. CHERRY OWEN : *See that smudge on the wall by the picture of Auntie Blossom? That's where you threw the sago. You only missed me by an inch.*

CHERRY OWEN : *I always miss Auntie Blossom too.*

MRS. CHERRY OWEN : *Remember last night? In you reeled, my boy, as drunk as a deacon with a big wet bucket and a fish-frail full of stout and you looked at me and you said, ` God has come home! ' you said, and then over the bucket you went, sprawling and bawling, and the floor was all flagons and eels.*

She serves her husband the stew.

CHERRY OWEN : *Was I wounded?*

MRS. CHERRY OWEN : *And then you took off your trousers and you said, `Does anybody want a fight!' Oh, you old baboon.*

CHERRY OWEN : *Give me a kiss.*

They kiss with great warmth and joy.

MRS. CHERRY OWEN : *And then you sang `Bread of Heaven',* *tenor and bass.*

CHERRY OWEN : *I always sing' Bread of Heaven. '*

As she walks back to pick up another saucepan, Mrs. Cherry Owen steps on an eel, forgotten from last night. She screams and throws it on the table.

Cherry Owen roars with laughter.

Then Mrs. Cherry Owen continues to the stove to pick up a saucepan full of leeks.

MRS. CHERRY OWEN : *And then you did a little dance on the table.*

CHERRY OWEN : *I did?*

MRS. CHERRY OWEN : *Drop dead!*

CHERRY OWEN : *And then what did I do?*

MRS. CHERRY OWEN : *Then you cried like a baby and said you were a poor drunk orphan with nowhere to go but the grave.*

CHERRY OWEN : *And what did I do next, my dear?*

Now Mrs. Cherry Owen serves her husband with the leeks.

MRS. CHERRY OWEN : *Then you danced on the table all over again and said you were King Solomon and I was your Mrs. Sheba.*

CHERRY OWEN : *And then?*

MRS. CHERRY OWEN : *And then I got you into bed and you snored all night like a brewery.*

Cherry Owen brings up a leek speared on a fork and bites it. Both laugh delightedly together.

Seen through the window full of meat, the First Voice sniffs the delicious smell coming from the butcher's shop.

FIRST VOICE : *From Beynon Butchers in Coronation Street, the smell of fried liver sidles out with onions on its breath . . .*

The First Voice puts out his hand to the Second Voice, who produces from his pocket one half-eaten apple. The First Voice refuses the offer and walks off. In the kitchen of the Beynons, the great black cat stands on the table, while Mrs. Beynon feeds it with liver from her plate. The cat's tail almost obscures the butcher himself, while Lily Smalls works at the sink in the background. (The scene is shot and cut formally in a group and single shots.)

MRS. BEYNON : *She likes the liver, Ben.*

MR. BEYNON : *She ought to do, Bess. It's her brother's.*

Mrs. Beynon screams and pushes away her plate.

MRS. BEYNON : *Oh, d'you hear that, Lily?*

LILY SMALLS : *Yes, mum.*

MRS. BEYNON : *We're eating pusscat.*

LILY SMALLS : *Yes, mum.*

MRS. BEYNON : *Oh, you cat-butcher!*

MR. BEYNON : *It was doctored, ,mind.*

MRS. BEYNON : *What's that got to do with it?*

MR. BEYNON : *Yesterday we had mole.*

MRS. BEYNON : *Oh, Lily, Lily!*

MR. BEYNON : *Monday, otter. Tuesday, mice.*

Mrs. Beynon screams.

LILY SMALLS : *Go on, Mrs. Beynon. He's the biggest liar in town.*

MRS. BEYNON : *Don't you dare say that about Mr. Beynon.*

LILY SMALLS : *Everybody knows it, mum.*

MRS. BEYNON : *Mr. Beynon never tells a lie. Do you, Ben?*

MR. BEYNON : *No, Bess. And now I am going out after the corgis, woof, woof, with my little cleaver.*

He leaves, making a chopping motion with his hand.

MRS. BEYNON : *Oh, Lily, Lily!*

On the quayside, two Fishermen repair their nets, complaining about the sun and the still calm sea.

FIRST FISHERMAN : *Nogood's risking it today.*

SECOND FISHERMAN : *There's bound to be a gale.*

We pan and tilt down to Nogood Boyo, stuck in shallow water and rowing hard in his messy dinghy, the *Zanzibar.*

NOGOOD BOYO : *I don't care if it is blowing a gale. This boyo's up to no good. I don't know who's up there and I don't care.*

Pan up with his look across the quiet bay to the greenlathered hill beyond and the fleecy clouds in the blue calm sky. There is a clap of thunder, an answer to Nogood's boasting.

Outside the pub, the First Voice nods at the Second Voice. They walk firmly into the bar. Ominous music sounds.

In the bar, Sinbad Sailors, grandson of Mary Ann Sailors, stands drawing a pint of bitter, as the First and the Second Voices come in. He seems to be talking to himself.

SECOND VOICE : *Is it opening time then?*

SINBAD SAILORS : *It's half-past eleven.*

SECOND VOICE: *It's been half-past eleven here for fifty years.*

SINBAD SAILORS : *It's always opening time at the Sailor's Arms. Buy me a pint?*

The First Voice does not move, while the Second Voice turns out one pocket.

SECOND VOICE : *Buy me one.*

Sinbad is seen drinking his pint alone behind the bar.

SINBAD SAILORS : *Here's to me, Sinbad Sailors.*

In Willy Nilly the Postman's back garden, the hens twitch and grieve for their slops, as Willy Nilly rumbles handily on, swilling down his tea from a mug, then throwing the leaves to them. He goes in at his kitchen door. Inside the kitchen, a coven of kettles stands on the hissing hot range. Behind them, Mrs. Willy Nilly is steaming a letter open. Willy Nilly enters and gives her more of the day's letters to read.

In the town square, three of the Neighbour women push out broken prams that bounce on the cobbles. In the prams are babies, chuckling at the motion. Three prams collide simultaneously. The babies begin to yell. P.C. Attila Rees looks on, smiling and swinging his truncheon.

FIRST NEIGHBOUR : *Look where you're going.*

SECOND NEIGHBOUR : *That pram should be tested.*

THIRD NEIGHBOUR : *I'll call a policeman* (looking at P.C. Rees). *Not you.*

In the overgrown garden outside Polly Garter's hovel, her Grandfather is sitting in an old pram under a clothes-line pegged with dancing and dripping underclothes. He shakes his head at the drips, and hears the baby at Polly's breast crying, as she pegs more washing on the line.

POLLY'S GRANDFATHER : *I want my pipe and he wants his bottle.*

There is the sound of a school-bell ringing, and we cut quickly to Mr. Pugh furiously ringing the school-bell.

A mother pushing off a small boy and girl from a cottage doorway.

A small girl having her nose wiped as she is shoved out. A mother hurrying away a little boy with his satchel.

Another small boy having his ginger hair smartened as he walks by his granny.

Now we see many small children running up the quayside along the Cockle Row of cottages. They turn up Coronation Street under Captain Cat's Schooner House on their way to school.

VOICES : *You're late for school, Albie . . . late for school . . .*

In the butcher's shop, Lily Smalls is scrubbing the marble counter, while Butcher Beynon rushes over to the inner door to pull aside a joint on a hook out of the way of the trim Gossamer Beynon on her way to teach at the school. She sulkily avoids her father's kiss, as she walks off.

GOSSAMER BEYNON : *Late for school.*

Lily looks after Gossamer in admiration.

LILY SMALLS : *There's education.*

Butcher Beynon goes back to the meat behind the counter, mincing like his daughter.

BUTCHER BEYNON : *Best trotters and mince.*

A Ministry Inspector in black suit and bowler hat suddenly appears behind the counter. He points disapprovingly at the mess of meat on the marble.

INSPECTOR : *What's this?*

BUTCHER BEYNON : *Owlmeat . . . Dog's eyes . . . Manchop!*

He throws the chop away over his shoulder.

As he walks forwards from the back of his shipshape room, Captain Cat feels at an Eskimo sculpture of a walrus. He stops at his open porthole on Coronation Street to hear all the morning of the town. Distant, the sound of children fighting in the playground.

CAPTAIN CAT to himself : *Maggie Richards, Ricky Rhys, Tommy Powell, our Sal, little Gerwain, Billy Swansea with the dog's voice, one of Mr. Waldo's, nasty Humphrey, Jackie with the sniff . . . Where's Dicky's Albie? And the boys from Ty-pant? Perhaps they got the rash again.*

There is a sudden cry among the children's voices.

As Captain Cat talks, intercut to Mr. Pugh angrily ringing his bell, then cut again to ...

Gossamer Beynon with her bell, as she tries vainly to separate the heap of fighting, yelling children.

GOSSAMER BEYNON : *Stop it, Stop it! Boys, stop it! Billy Swansea! Now get inside the lot of you!*

Her accent is no longer refined. Intercut with Captain Cat, as he walks away from his porthole to sit slowly in his chair facing the sun and the sea.

CAPTAIN CAT : *Somebody's hit Maggie Richards. Two to one it's Billy Swansea. Never trust a boy who barks.*

There is a burst of barking.

CAPTAIN CAT : *Right again! It's Billy. Better put a book down your trousers.*

The children's voices die away, to be replaced by the soft rat-tat-tat on a door. Captain Cat is now standing in front of his chair at his open sunny window on the sea.

CAPTAIN CAT : *That's Willy Nilly knocking at Bay View .*

Outside the spruce porch of Bay View, Willy Nilly, the postman, knocks softly at the door. The knocker hardly makes any sound and he skids on the slippery steps.

CAPTAIN CAT'S VOICE : *Rat-tat-tat, very soft. The knocker's got a kid glove on.*

Back to Captain Cat, standing by his window.

CAPTAIN CAT : *Who's sent a letter to Mrs. Ogmore-Pritchard?*

On the red-and-black squares of the steps, Willy Nilly's boots skid as if his ankles were roller-skates. Throughout his scene with Mrs. Ogmore-Pritchard, he fights to keep his balance.

CAPTAIN CAT'S VOICE : *Careful now, she swabs the front glassy . . .*

During his commentary, the old sailor gradually eases himself into his high-backed wooden chair.

CAPTAIN CAT : *Every step's like a bar of soap. Mind your size twelveses. That old Bessie would beeswax the lawn to make the birds slip.*

> The door of Bay View opens to reveal the formidable Mrs. Ogmore-Pritchard, broom at the ready to sweep away intruders. Seen from front and back, the postman slips on the tiles.

WILLY NILLY : *Morning, Mrs. Ogmore-Pritchard.*

MRS. OGMORE-PRITCHARD : *Good morning, postman.*

WILLY NILLY : *Here's a letter for you with stamped and addressed envelope enclosed, all the way from Builth Wells. A gentleman wants to study birds and can he have accommodation for two weeks and a bath vegetarian.*

MRS. OGMORE-PRITCHARD : *No.*

WILLY NILLY : *You wouldn't know he was in the house, Mrs. Ogmore-Pritchard. He'd be out in the mornings at the bang of dawn with his bag of breadcrumbs and his little telescope. . .*

MRS OGMORE-PRITCHARD : *And come home at all hours covered with feathers. I don't want persons in my nice clean rooms breathing all over the chairs . . .*

WILLY NILLY : *Cross my heart, he won't breathe.*

MRS. OGMORE-PRITCHARD : . . . *And putting their feet on my carpets and sneezing on my china and sleeping in my sheets . . .*

WILLY NILLY : *He only wants a* single *bed, Mrs. Ogmore-Pritchard.*

> As Mrs. Ogmore-Pritchard slams the door in his face, Willy Nilly falls backwards on the tiles, laughing.
> Captain Cat is now seated, as he listens to the familiar noises of the postman's round.

CAPTAIN CAT : *And back she goes to the kitchen to polish the potatoes. And on Willy Nilly goes to clatter the cobbles . . .*

> Now we see Willy Nilly's boots as they climb the slate steps up to a cottage door, where Mrs. Rose Cottage stands, waiting for her letter.

CAPTAIN CAT'S VOICE : . . . *That's Mrs. Rose Cottage. What's today?*

MRS. ROSE COTTAGE : *What's today?*

> The old Captain seems to delight in knowing what they will say before they say it.

CAPTAIN CAT : *To-day she gets the letter from her sister in Gorslas.*

Willy Nilly tells Mrs. Rose Cottage about her letter.

WILLY NILLY : *To-day you get the letter from your sister in Gorslas.*

Captain Cat knows what Mrs. Rose Cottage will ask.

CAPTAIN CAT : *How's the twin's teeth?*

Mrs. Rose Cottage looks after Willy Nilly, as he clomps off.

MRS. ROSE COTTAGE : *How's the twin's teeth?*

WILLY NILLY mouthing to camera : *Terrible.*

Willy Nilly goes off down the sunny hill towards the town, commenting to an old woman in her doorway.

WILLY NILLY : *Nothing for you today, love . . . The twin's teeth, terrible ...*

Back at Captain Cat's window, the old blind man is still listening.

CAPTAIN CAT : *That's the emporium.*

Willy Nilly comes up to Mog Edwards, still waiting at the doorway of his haberdasher's.

WILLY NILLY : *Morning, Mr. Edwards. Very small news. Mrs. Ogmore-Pritchard won't have birds in the house, and Mr. Pugh's bought a book now on how to do in Mrs. Pugh.*

MOG EDWARDS : *Have you got a letter from* her?

As Willy Nilly tells Mog what is in Myfanwy's letter, he keeps the letter away from Mog's snatching fingers.

WILLY NILLY : *Miss Price loves you with all her heart. Smelling of lavender to-day. She's down to the last of the elderflower wine but the quince jam's bearing up and she's knitting roses on the doilies. Last week she sold three jars of boiled sweets, pound of humbugs, half a box of jellybabies, and six coloured photos of Llaregyb. Yours for ever. Then twenty-one X's.*

Mog snatches Myfanwy's letter, and gives Willy Nilly his letter to her.

MOG EDWARDS : *Oh, Willy Nilly, she's a ruby! Here's my letter. Put it into her hands now.*

Willy Nilly takes the letter and leaves Mog clutching Myfanwy's letter to his bosom.

Captain Cat is still listening to the postman's further steps.

CAPTAIN CAT : *He's stopping at School House.*

As Willy Nilly approaches Mrs. Pugh standing on her doorstep outside School House, we hear Gossamer Beynon's voice from the School.

GOSSAMER BEYNON'S VOICE : *Now, children, I think it's time you learned your four times table . . .*

Seen from over their shoulders and in close-up, Willy Nilly and Mrs. Pugh have their confrontation over the parcel.

WILLY NILLY : *Morning Mrs. Pugh. Mrs. Ogmore-Pritchard won't have a gentleman in from Builth Wells because he'll sleep in her sheets, Mrs. Rose Cottage's sister in Gorslas's twins have got to have them out .. .*

MRS. PUGH : *Give me the parcel.*

She snatches it out of his hand and begins ripping it open.

WILLY NILLY : *It's for* Mr. *Pugh, Mrs. Pugh.*

MRS. PUGH *: Never you mind. What's inside it?*

WILLY NILLY : *A book called* Lives of the Great Poisoners.

He runs off very fast, as Mrs. Pugh looks furiously after him.

GOSSAMER BEYNON'S VOICE :

Nine fours are thirty-six. Ten fours are forty.

Captain Cat now hears quicker feet hurrying along the quayside.

CAPTAIN CAT : *Mr. Waldo hurrying to the Sailor's Arms. Pint of stout with an egg in it . . . There's a letter for him.*

Willy Nilly is indeed waiting for Mr. Waldo outside the Sailor's Arms. He hands him a long envelope.

WILLY NILLY : *It's another paternity suit, Mr. Waldo.*

Mr. Waldo hurries across the cobbles and . . . Into the pub, calling out in desperation.

MR. WALDO : *Quick, Sinbad. Pint of stout. And no egg in it.*

Ominous music sounds as the First and Second Voices get up from the bar and leave the pub . . . And walk onto the quayside, where they stop and look back. At Cat's window, a troubled look crosses the old Captain's face.

CAPTAIN CAT : *Who are those then? What are they looking for?*

Outside the Sailor's Arms, the two Voices walk away. The music fades.

Captain Cat's face relaxes as the sound of women's feet in Coronation Street rises more and more.

CAPTAIN CAT : *All the women are out this morning, in the sun. You can tell it's spring. Who's that talking by the pump? Talking flatfish.*

In the town square, a Fisherman leans on the handle that dribbles water, as he talks to the women around the pump.

CAPTAIN CAT'S VOICE : *What can you talk about flatfish?*

Cut back to Captain Cat in his chair.

CAPTAIN CAT : *That's Mrs. Dai Bread One, waltzing up the street like a jelly, every time she shakes . . .*

Mrs. Dai Bread One comes up on Mrs. Butcher Beynon outside the meat shop. The butcher's wife wears a mauve jumper and holds her great black cat.

CAPTAIN CAT'S VOICE : *. . . It's slap, slap, slap.*

MRS. DAI BREAD ONE : *What did you have for breakfast this morning? Pig snout?*

Mrs. Butcher Beynon looks annoyed.

Back to Captain Cat at his window, as he listens, smiling.

CAPTAIN CAT : *Who's that? Mrs. Butcher Beynon with her pet black cat, it follows her everywhere, miaow and all.*

Now the old Captain is seen in profile, his red-veined nose prominent.

CAPTAIN CAT : *There goes Mrs. Twenty-Three, important.*

On the quayside, the stout Mrs. Twenty-Three is seen interviewing another housewife, as Cat looks down on them.

CAPTAIN CAT : *The sun gets up and goes down in her dewlap. When she shuts her eyes, it's night.*

On the other side of the harbour among the beached boats, the pretty and young Mae Rose Cottage pulls along two goats on a rope, followed by a small white kid. She wears a thin dress and silly high heels. Beyond her across the water, we see Schooner House.

CAPTAIN CAT'S VOICE : *High heels now, in the morning too.*

Cut back to Cat, hearing with his eyes at his open window.

CAPTAIN CAT : *Mrs. Rose Cottage's eldest Mae, seventeen and never been kissed ho ho . . .*

Now we are close on the back legs of a reluctant nannygoat being dragged forwards, followed by its kid, flicking its ears.

CAPTAIN CAT'S VOICE : *. . . Going young and milking under my window. . .*

From his chair, Cat fondly comments.

CAPTAIN CAT : *. . . To the field with the nannygoats. She reminds me all the way. Can't hear what the women are gabbing round the pump . . .*

Round the pump, the women settle down for their chat between their shopping errands.

CAPTAIN CAT'S VOICE : *Same as ever.*

Back on Cat, as he hears the milk-cart pass.

CAPTAIN CAT : *Ocky Milkman on his round. I will say this, his milk's as fresh as the dew. Half dew it is . . .*

On the sound of organ music, we show the ginger Organ Morgan playing at his portable organ.

CAPTAIN CAT'S VOICE : *Organ Morgan's at it early. You can tell it's spring.*

Back now to Captain Cat as he listens closely.

CAPTAIN CAT : *Somebody's coming. Now the voices round the pump can see somebody coming. Hush, there's a hush! You can tell by the noise of the hush, it's Polly Garter.*

Cut on his words to a shot of Polly Garter wearing her shawl, as she swaggers past the cherry tree in the town square and past the women by the pump, who glare after her in an angry hush, before breaking into their comments.

FIRST NEIGHBOUR : *She's having a baby.*

SECOND NEIGHBOUR : *She's having us on.*

THIRD NEIGHBOUR : *Just needs a slimming.*

FOURTH NEIGHBOUR : *But that Polly Garter . . .*

FIRST HOUSEWIFE : *Giving her belly an airing.*

SECOND HOUSEWIFE : *There should be a law.*

THIRD HOUSEWIFE : *Seen Mrs. Beynon's new mauve jumper?*

FOURTH HOUSEWIFE : *It's her old grey one dyed.*

FIFTH HOUSEWIFE : *Who's died?*

FIRST NEIGHBOUR : *Nobody's dying.*

SECOND NEIGHBOUR : *There's a lovely day.*

THIRD NEIGHBOUR : *Oh, the cost of soapflakes!*

As the women burst into their gabble again, we come back to the smiling old Cat.

CAPTAIN CAT : *Hullo, Polly, who's there?*

We see Polly Garter strutting on the sunny quayside, as she looks up smiling at Cat's window. The passing P.C. Attila Rees lifts his helmet to her, hoping nobody is noticing.

POLLY GARTER : *Me, love.*

She walks off, back to her washing and her babies.

Captain Cat is delighted at his window.

CAPTAIN CAT : That's *Polly Garter! Hullo, Polly my love, can you hear the dumb goose-hiss of the wives as they huddle and peck or flounce at a waddle away?*

Back at the pump, we slowly pan across the faces of the gossiping housewives, then pull away to show the group.

CAPTAIN CAT'S VOICE : *Who cuddled you when? Which of their gandering hubbies moaned in Milk Wood for your naughty mothering arms and body like a wardrobe, love?*

Again we watch Cat, now seen from above, as he comments on the wives' comments on Polly.

CAPTAIN CAT : *Scrub the floors of the Welfare Hall for the Mothers' Union Social Dance, you're one mother won't wriggle her roly poly bum or pat her fat little buttery feet in that wedding-ringed holy tonight.*

We hear a cock crow.

CAPTAIN CAT : *Too late, cock, too late.*

On his look of regret, we cut to. . .

Coronation Street, outside an old NAAFI hut, where the Two Voices approach, looking expectant.

SECOND VOICE : *The town's half over with its morning.*

The men stop happily. They see what they are looking for.

SECOND VOICE : *The morning's busy as bees.*

From their point of view, we see Norma Jane Jenkins as she sashays down the street. She is dressed in the style fit-to-kill of the forties (and the seventies) - wedge shoes, padded shoulders, red red ringlets, red red mouth. She is the Rita Hayworth of Llaregyb. Feeling the presence of the two men who are waiting for her, she shortens her pace, but smiles to see them.

SECOND VOICE : *Norma Jane . . . Norma Jane . . .*

A series of quick shots shows the encounter of Norma Jane with the two men, as she slips into the First Voice's hug and goes off with the pair.

FIRST VOICE : *There's the clip clop of horses on the sunhoneyed cobbles of the humming streets, hammering of horseshoes, gobble quack and cackle, tomtit twitter from the bird-ounced boughs, braying on Donkey Down. Bread is baking, pigs are grunting, chop goes the butcher, milk-churns bell, tills ring, sheep cough, dogs shout, saws sing . . .*

Now the First Voice is pulling the laughing Norma Jane down a path by bleating goats, with the Second Voice tagging on after.

FIRST VOICE : *Oh, the Spring whinny and morning moo from the clog dancing farms, the gulls' gab and rabble . . .*

By the side of the Dewi River, Mae Rose Cottage pulls her goats away from the town towards the pasture.

FIRST VOICE : *. . . On the boat-bobbing river and sea and the cockles bubbling in the sand . . .*

Now the two men and Norma Jane are small figures, as they move along Heron Head towards the sea.

FIRST VOICE : *. . . Scamper of sanderlings, curlew cry, crow caw, pigeon coo, clock strike, bull bellow . . .*

Now we are back in the town square as a housewife, the First
Woman of the next scene, moves over from the pump to the
general shop.

FIRST VOICE : . . . *And the ragged gabble of the beargarden
school as the women scratch and babble in Mrs. Organ Morgan's
general shop where everything is sold : custard, buckets, henna,
rat-traps, shrimp-nets, sugar, stamps, confetti, paraffin, hatchets,
whistles.*

Inside the general shop with Mrs. Organ Morgan behind the
counter, a babble of women chatter and pull and peek and pry
everywhere, while the First Woman starts off a new round of
gossip.

FIRST WOMAN : *Mrs. Ogmore-Pritchard . . .*

SECOND WOMAN : *La di da . . .*

FIRST WOMAN : *Got a man in Builth Wells . . .*

THIRD WOMAN : *And he got a little telescope to look at birds.*

Behind their voices, we hear the sound of an organ playing its
counterpoint.

SECOND WOMAN : *Willy Nilly said . . .*

THIRD WOMAN : *Remember her first husband? He didn't need a
telescope.*

FIRST WOMAN : *He looked at them undressing through the key-
hole.*

THIRD WOMAN : *And he used to shout Tallyho!*

SECOND WOMAN : *But Mr. Ogmore was a proper gentleman .*

FIRST WOMAN : *Even though he hanged his collie.*

THIRD WOMAN : *Seen Mrs. Butcher Beynon?*

SECOND WOMAN : *She said Butcher Beynon put dogs in the
mincer.*

FIRST WOMAN : *Go on, he's pulling her leg . . .*

THIRD WOMAN : *Now don't you dare tell her that, there's a
dear. . .*

SECOND WOMAN : *Or she'll think he's trying to pull it off and
eat it.*

FOURTH WOMAN : *There's a nasty lot live here when you come
to think.*

FIRST WOMAN : *Look at that Nogood Boyo now . . .*

SECOND WOMAN : *Too lazy to wipe his snout . . .*

THIRD WOMAN : *And going out fishing every day and all he ever brought back was a Mrs. Samuels . . .*

Mrs. Organ Morgan shakes her head at the news.

FIRST WOMAN : *Been in the water a week.*

SECOND WOMAN : *And look at Ocky Milkman's wife that nobody's ever seen . . .*

FIRST WOMAN : *He keeps her in the cupboard with the empties.*

THIRD WOMAN : *And think of Dai Bread with two wives.*

SECOND WOMAN : *One for the daytime one for the night.*

Now the organ music stops and Organ Morgan passes through the store behind the customers, his music sheets under his arm.

ORGAN MORGAN : *Hello, ladies.*

As he goes out, the women begin again, and the organ music.

FOURTH WOMAN : *Men are brutes on the quiet.*

THIRD WOMAN : *And how's Organ Morgan, Mrs. Morgan?*

FIRST WOMAN : *You look dead beat.*

SECOND WOMAN : *It's organ organ all time with him.*

THIRD WOMAN : *Up every night until midnight playing the organ.*

Mrs. Morgan shakes her head in a satisfied way.

MRS. ORGAN MORGAN : *Oh, I'm a martyr to music.*

In the infant school, Gossamer Beynon stands by a blackboard. On it is written

HARP

HYMN

ORGAN

which Gossamer has just finished chalking up. She turns to the infants.

GOSSAMER : *Organ.*

We pan down to a group of twenty Tots who begin to chant at their teacher.

TOTS : *Organ Morgan!*

Organ Morgan!

Gossamer flushes by the blackboard.

GOSSAMER : *I'll never be refeened if I twitch.*

From the attic window of the Sailor's Arms, the old Mary Ann Sailors looks at the sun. Organ music swells.

MARY ANN SAILORS : *It is Spring in Llaregyb in the sun in my old age . . .*

> The quayside and harbour are honey and curds in the morning sun, while the notes of the organ swell like grapes.

MARY ANN SAILORS : *. . . And this is the Chosen Land . . .*

> In front of the range of hissing kettles in her kitchen, Mrs. Willy Nilly steams open Mog Edwards' letter to Myfanwy Price. A slice of sun tries to get through the grimy glass and steam in the pygmy kitchen where Willy Nilly sits, drinking his black black tea as he listens.

MRS. WILLY NILLY : *From the Emporium, Llaregyb. Sole Prop Mr. Mog Edwards. Beloved Myfanwy Price my Bride in Heaven . . .*

> Cut to Mog Edwards outside his emporium, pressing Myfanwy's letter to his heart.

MOG EDWARDS VOICE : *I love you until Death do us part and then we shall be together for ever and ever .. .*

> Now the emporium is streaming with thousands of ribbons in every colour. On an armchair, Mog Edwards sits in his full formal shop clothes; but on his lap is the wet and nestling Myfanwy Price, dressed in a scaly evening dress with a train that shakes like a mermaid's tail.

MOG EDWARDS VOICE : *I dreamed last night you were all dripping wet and you sat on my lap as the Reverend Jenkins went down the street. I see you got a mermaid in your lap he said and he lifted his hat. He is a proper Christian. Not like Cherry Owen who said you should have thrown her back he said.*

Now Mog is mouthing the cups of a brassiere filled with money and lifting up a display leg to kiss, while more money pours out of this cornucopia.

MOG EDWARDS VOICE : *Business is very poorly. Polly Garter bought two garters with roses but she never got stockings so what is the use I say. Mr. Waldo tried to sell me a woman's nightie outsize he said he found it and we know where. If this goes on I shall be in the workhouse.*

In the middle of a grey bower on pink rosettes, Mog Edwards and Myfanwy Price lovingly entwine. We pull back to show they are framed by a large red cut-out of a heart, frilled and pretty.

MOG EDWARDS VOICE : *My heart is in your bosom and yours in mine. God be with you always Myfanwy Price and keep you lovely for me in His Heavenly Mansion. I must stop now and remain, Your Eternal, Mog Edwards.*

Back in the steaming kitchen, Mrs. Willy Nilly avidly finishes reading the letter.

MRS. WILLY NILLY : *And then a little message with a rubber stamp. Shop at Mog's!!*

Willy Nilly rises, belching.

WILLY NILLY : *Got to go to the House of Commons.*

The postman comes out into his back garden, goes to the outhouse, dislodges a hen, and enters. Now we pan up and over the roofs of the town to the rolling hill above, yellow with gorse.

On Donkey Down, Norma Jane laughs between the two men, as they walk between grazing donkeys on a grassy slope above the sunny sea.

FIRST VOICE : *Outside, the sun springs down on the rough and tumbling town. It runs through the hedges of Goosegog Lane, cuffing the birds to sing. Spring whips green in Milk Wood. Llaregyb this snip of a morning is wildfruit and warm, the streets, fields, sand and waters springing in the young sun. Donkeys angelically drowse on Donkey Down . . .*

SECOND VOICE : *Norma Jane. . .*

On a red tractor, a young farmer drives forwards ploughing.

Gulls hover and pounce on the worm-rich furrows.

FIRST VOICE : *Herring gulls heckling down to the harbour where the fishermen spit and prop the morning up and eye the fishy sea smooth to the sea's end as it lulls in blue. Green and gold money, tobacco, tinned salmon, hats with feathers, pots of fish-paste . . .*

Now we see Nogood Boyo rowing into the shallows of the bay, while the gulls fly off in the opposite direction.

FIRST VOICE : *. . . Warmth for the winter-to-be, wave and leap in it rich and slippery in the flash and shapes of fishes through the cold sea-streets. But. with blue lazy eyes the fishermen gaze at that milk-maid whispering water with no ruck or ripple . . .*

We move from the flying gulls across the harbour to where the two Fishermen sit repairing their nets on the quay.

FIRST VOICE : *. . . As though it blew great guns and serpents and typhooned the town.*

FIRST FISHERMAN : *Too rough for fishing to-day.*

SECOND FISHERMAN : *Thank God.*

The fishermen spit gobs at the sea-gulls, then turn to walk, rolling and slow, to the pub. Behind them, Schooner House.

In his chair in Schooner House, Captain Cat rages in a day-dream.

CAPTAIN CAT : *No, I'll take the mulatto, by God, who's Captain here? Parlez-vous jig jig, Madam?*

Outside Cat's window, where he now sits listening to the naughty forfeiting children tumble and rhyme on the cobbles, the older children play at their singing and kissing game, dancing in a circle round Gwennie in the middle.

GIRLS' VOICES :

> *Gwennie call the boys*
> *They make such a noise.*

GWENNIE :

> *Boys boys boys*
> *Come along to me.*

Norma Jane and the two men are coming gaily up to a hut on a seapoint. In the background, bullocks and goats graze.

Norma Jane leads the way into the hut. The First Voice pushes the Second Voice away from the door as he follows the girl in; but the Second Voice dashes inside after them.

GIRLS' VOICES :

> *Boys boys boys*
> *Kiss Gwennie where she says*
> *Or give her a penny.*
> *Go on, Gwennie.*

GWENNIE'S VOICE :

> *Kiss me on Llaregyb Hill*
> *Or give me a penny.*

Now we are inside the hut. The First Voice hugs Norma Jane and begins unbuttoning the jacket of her trouser-suit. Laughing, she pushes away his fumbling fingers and undoes her own jacket and takes off her scarf, which she hands to the Second Voice. Eagerly, the First Voice pulls his jacket off.

GWENNIE'S VOICE : *What's your name?*

JOHNNIE CRISTO'S VOICE : *Johnnie Cristo.*

GWENNIE'S VOICE :

> *Kiss me on Llaregyb Hill Johnnie Cristo*
> *Or give me a penny mister.*

JOHNNIE CRISTO'S VOICE :

> *Gwennie Gwennie*
> *I kiss you on Llaregyb Hill.*
> *Now I haven't got to give you a penny.*

On the quayside, the boys and girls still dance in a ring round the knowing Gwennie under Captain Cat's window.

GIRLS' VOICES :

> *Boys boys boys*
> *Kiss Gwennie where she says*
> *Or give her a penny.*
> *Go on, Gwennie.*

In the hut, the First Voice pulls Norma Jane onto her knees, then onto the ground.

We move off them with the Second Voice, as he takes her jacket and scarf away and tries to hang them on a nail in the corner of the hut. He looks back, lust on his thin face.

GWENNIE'S VOICE :

> *Kiss me in Milk Wood*
> *Or give me a penny.*
> *What's your name?*

DICKY'S VOICE : *Dicky.*

GWENNIE'S VOICE :

> *Kiss me in Milk Wood Dicky*
> *Or give me a penny quickly.*

DICKY'S VOICE : *Gwennie Gwennie . . .*

Back on the quayside, Dicky is scared and shy, as Gwennie confronts him.

DICKY :

> *. . . I can't kiss you in Milk Wood.*

GIRLS' VOICES :

> *Gwennie ask him why.*

GWENNIE : *Why?*

DICKY : *Because my mother says I mustn't.*

Now we see Gwennie, backed by the accusing ring of girls and boys.

GIRLS' VOICES :

> *Cowardy cowardy custard*
> *Give Gwennie a penny.*

GWENNIE : *Give me a penny.*

Back to Dicky, as he still refuses to hand over.

DICKY : *I haven't got any.*

The boys and girls now surround Dicky and begin beating at him.

GIRLS' VOICES :

> *Put him in the river*
> *Up to his liver*
> *Quick quick Dirty Dick*
> *Beat him on the bum*
> *With a rhubarb stick.*
> *Aiee!*

The shrill girls giggle and squeal as they clutch and thrash Dicky, and he blubbers away down the quayside, pursued by the gang.

The Second Voice is now putting Norma Jane's scarf in his mouth and sucking it, as he watches . . . The First Voice lying above the near-naked Norma Jane and kissing her on the floor of the hut. We can still hear the noise of the running children.

The boys and girls are still pursuing Dicky, who escapes past Myfanwy Price's sweetshop, while the rest of the children run inside. Behind the counter, Miss Price tries to cope with the gaggle and giggle of children, as they get at the sweets, crushing the tots already there up to the counter. Behind Myfanwy Price are bright jars of humbugs, gobstoppers big as wens, hundreds and thousands . . .

MYFANWY PRICE : *And what do you want then? . . . What is it you want?*

The children screech and clutch for their sweets offering pennies to Miss Price, and we see . . .

Two girls, smiling and sucking at their liquorice . . .

Myfanwy handing out humbugs and taking coins . . .

A small boy pulling at his rubbery sweet . . .

A tiny girl wedged up against the counter, as she sucks at her red lollipop. Above her, children's hands grab for sweets and hold out more money.

MRS. DAI BREAD TWO'S VOICE : *Cross my palm with silver, Mrs. One .. .*

Cut from the children handing over their pennies to the front gate of the Dai Bread cottage, where Mrs. Dai Bread One and Mrs. Dai Bread Two sit, one plumply and one darkly blooming. Mrs. Dai Bread Two is looking into a crystal ball which she holds in the lap of her dirty red petticoat, hard against her hard dark thighs. We move slowly in on the pair of them as they talk, while Lily Smalls bicycles by with the washing.

MRS. DAI BREAD TWO : . . . *Out of our housekeeping money. Aah!*

MRS. DAI BREAD ONE : *What d'you see, lovie?*

MRS. DAI BREAD TWO : *I see a featherbed. With three pillows on it. And a text above the bed. I can't see what it says, there's great clouds blowing . . . Now they have blown away. God is Love, the text says.*

MRS. DAI BREAD ONE : *That's our bed.*

MRS. DAI BREAD TWO : *And now it's vanished . . . The sun's spinning like a top. Who's this coming out of the sun?*

Now we see inside the crystal ball, held on Mrs. Dai Bread Two's scarlet lap between her scarlet nails.

MRS. DAI BREAD TWO'S VOICE : *It's a hairy little man with big pink lips.*

MRS. DAI BREAD ONE'S VOICE : *It's Dai; it's Dai Bread!*

Indeed, we are now watching Dai Bread in his nightshirt, throwing away his boots, beating his chest with his fists, and climbing into a feather bed below a text which says GOD IS LOVE. He climbs in between both of his wives, looking at each, whistles through his teeth, opens both arms, and grabs.

MRS. DAI BREAD TWO'S VOICE : *Ssh! The featherbed's floating back. The little man's taking his boots off. He's pulling his shirt over his head. He's beating his chest with his fists. He's climbing into bed.*

MRS. DAI BREAD ONE'S VOICE : *Go on, go on.*

MRS. DAI BREAD TWO'S VOICE : *There's two women in bed. He looks at them both, with his head cocked on one side. He's whistling through his teeth. Now he grips his little arms round one of the women.*

MRS. DAI BREAD ONE'S VOICE : *Which one, which one?*

Actually we see in the crystal ball Dai Bread grabbing at his second wife, but we cut back to . . .

The two women in front of their cottage, as Mrs. Dai Bread Two looks up in triumph from her crystal ball.

MRS. DAI BREAD TWO *: I can't see any more. There's great clouds blowing again.*

MRS. DAI BREAD ONE : *Ach, the mean old clouds!*

At that moment, Dai Bread comes up behind the women and puts his head between his wives so that each can plant a kiss on his cheek.

Outside the Welfare Hall in Coronation Street, the Reverend Eli Jenkins hurries past on his morning calls with his umbrella and his basket full of jellies, then stops to hear the sound of singing.

POLLY GARTER'S VOICE :

I loved a man whose name was Tom
He was strong as a bear and two yards long . . .

ELI JENKINS raptly: *Eisteddfoddai!*

Inside the Welfare Hall, we move slowly in on Polly Garter, as she scrubs the floor for the Mothers' Union Dance that the banners declare on the wall of the creaky old hall. She scrubs in lovely sudsy circles in an orgy of white curves.

POLLY GARTER singing :

I loved a man whose name was Dick
He was big as a barrel and three feet thick
And I loved a man whose name was Harry
Six feet tall and sweet as a cherry
But the one I loved best awake or asleep
Was little Willy Wee and he's six feet deep .. .

In the hut, the First Voice kisses Norma Jane down her flank, then up again to her face. She stretches in ecstacy.

POLLY GARTER'S VOICE :

> *O Tom Dick and Harry were three fine men*
> *And I'll never have such loving again*
> *But little Willy Wee who took me on his knee*
> *Little Willy Wee was the man for me .. .*

Now we see the watching Second Voice, as he slips off his overcoat and squats, looking, looking.

POLLY GARTER'S VOICE :

> *Now men from every parish round*
> *Run after me and roll me on the ground . . .*

We now see the First Voice kissing Norma Jane again.

POLLY GARTER'S VOICE :

> *But whenever I love another man back*
> *Johnnie from the Hill or Sailing Jack*
> *I always think as they do what they please*
> *Of Tom Dick and Harry who were tall as trees . . .*

As the white jersey of the First Voice moves over the body of Norma Jane, we cut to Polly Garter's hands, scrubbing the floor in soapy curves, then we tilt up to her face.

POLLY GARTER :

> *And most I think when I'm by their side*
> *Of little Willy Wee who downed and died . . .*

In the hut, the First Voice is now beckoning the Second Voice, who is crawling up like a jackal at the lion's feast. The First Voice pushes Norma Jane across to his mate's embrace, although she looks at him in appeal.

POLLY GARTER'S VOICE :

> *O Tom Dick and Harry were three fine men*
> *And I'll never have such loving again*
> *But little Willy Wee who took me on his knee . . .*

Back in the Welfare Hall, we move from Polly on her knees, squeezing out a dirty rag in her pail, up to the window.

POLLY GARTER :

> *. . . Little Willy Weazel is the man for me.*

Outside in the street, The Reverend Eli Jenkins stands, listening to the last notes of Polly Garter's song die away.

ELI JENKINS : *Praise the Lord! We are a musical nation.*

He hurries off on his errands of mercy.

Back in the hut, we pull back from an out-of-focus shot of moving pinks like octopi undersea to show Norma Jane and the Second Voice twining, while the First Voice lies on his back, at his ease.

Ominous music sounds.

FIRST VOICE : *The town's as full as a lovebird's egg.*

Mr. Waldo looks out of the window of the Sailor's Arms at the Reverend Eli Jenkins saying his good mornings to two ladies hurrying past.

Now Mr. Waldo pulls his head back inside the pub.

MR. WALDO : *There goes the Reverend with his brolly and his odes.*

He downs the rest of his mug of stout in one long swallow, then walks towards the, bar, where Sinbad Sailors stands. The two silent Fishermen prop up the bar, flushing down their pints.

MR. WALDO : *Fill 'em up, Sinbad, I'm on the treacle to-day.*

Sinbad fills up his mug.

SINBAD SAILORS : *Oh Mr. Waldo, I dote on that Gossamer Beynon.*

In the infant class in the school, we track` behind the twenty Tots, who sit around the kneeling Gossamer Beynon, singing *Frère Jacques* in Welsh and clapping their hands. Back behind the bar of the pub, Sinbad Sailors grieves.

SINBAD SAILORS : *She's a lady all over.*

MR. WALDO : *No lady that I know is.*

Now Gossamer is trying to teach her Tots how to be refined. They repeat the words after her, very bored.

GOSSAMER BEYNON : *No, no, children, your eccents please.*

It was a lover and his lass

With a 'ey . . . With a hey and a ho and a hey nonny . . .

Back in the pub, we hear Gossamer's voice say 'no' to the lugubrious Sinbad behind the bar.

SINBAD SAILORS : *And if only grandma'd die and leave me the pub, cross my heart I'd go down on my knees Mr. Waldo and I'd say, Miss Gossamer I'd say . . .*

Backed by the blackboard in the schoolroom with two bigger girls, kept in for being naughty, Gossamer conducts as they sing

GOSSAMER AND GIRLS singing :

> *When birds do sing hey ding a ding a ding*
> *Sweet lovers love the Spring . . .*

In the Welfare Hall we see Polly Garter in close-up, still on her knees.

POLLY GARTER singing :

> *Tom Dick and Harry were three fine men*
> *And I'll never have such . . .*

LITTLE GIRLS' VOICES : *. . . Ding a ding . . .*

POLLY GARTER : *. . . Again.*

On the sunny quayside, Gossamer is now walking home from school. Her body moves and swings despite her prim walk, and the sun hums through her dress and buzzes in the honey of her body.

She passes the Sailor's Arms and the hot gaze of Mr. Waldo and Sinbad, staring out in lust and joy.

POLLY GARTER'S VOICE :

> *Tom Dick and Harry were three fine men*
> *And I'll never have such . . .*

LITTLE GIRLS' VOICES : *. . . Ding a ding. . .*

POLLY GARTER'S VOICE : . . . . *Again.*

Now we move before Gossamer, as she leaves the pub and the hot looks behind her. She speaks to camera.

GOSSAMER BEYNON : *I don't care if he is common . . . I want to gobble him up.*

Now we see Sinbad at his window, grieving with desire.

GOSSAMER'S VOICE : *I don't care if he* does *drop his aitches . . .*

Seen from Sinbad's imagination, Gossamer now wears only her pink pants and high heels, as she walks away down the steps into the Dewi River.

GOSSAMER'S VOICE : . . . *So long as he's all cucumber and hooves.*

At the pub window, Sinbad still sorrows.

SINBAD SAILORS : *Oh, Gossamer Beynon, why are you so proud?*

In his dream vision, the bare Gossamer vanishes down the steps into the Dewi River.

SINBAD'S VOICE : *Oh, beautiful beautiful Gossamer B* ....

Sinbad now begins to pull his fists back and forth, as if pumping his beer or her legs.

SINBAD SAILORS :

> *I wish I wish that you were for me.*
> *I wish you were not so educated. Gossamer . . .*
> *Gossamer. . .*

In the hut on the headland, the First Voice summons Norma Jane back to his arms, and she comes across and lies upon him, kissing him gratefully, while the Second Voice looks sadly on.

We hear the sound of young children singing.

CHILDREN'S SONG :

> *Johnnie Crack and Flossie Snail*
> *Kept their baby in a milking pail*
> *Flossie Snail and Johnnie Crack*
> *One would pull it out and one would put it back*
> *O it's my turn now said Flossie Snail*
> *To take the baby from the milking pail*
> *And it's my turn now said Johnnie Crack*
> *To smack it on the head and put it back . . .*

Now we are looking down on the quayside, as a group of little boys and girls chase an old car full of hens along the quay.

We follow them as they run and we tilt up the front of Schooner House to show Captain Cat leaning out of his window and smiling. The sun is bright on the green hill beyond. The old Captain sits back in his chair.

CHILDREN'S SONG :

> *Johnnie Crack and Flossie Snail*
> *Kept their baby in a milking pail*
> *One would put it back and one would pull it out*
> *And all it had to drink was ale and stout*
> *For Johnnie Crack and Flossie Snail*
> *Always used to say that stout and ale*
> *Was good for a baby in a milking pail . . .*

As the song ends, there is a woman's scream, and we cut to a line drawing of a lady shot by gunmen.

We pull back to show the dusty vault of the Pughs' dining-room. A book wrapped in a plain brown cover is on the table by Mr. Pugh. He underlines something in the book, while Mrs. Pugh looks at him in cold disapproval.

MRS. PUGH : *Persons with manners do not read at table, Pugh.*

She puts a digestive tablet as big as a horse-pill in her glass, then washes it down with water as cloudy as pea-soup.

MRS. PUGH : *Some persons were brought up in pigsties.*

Seen over his wife's shoulder, Mr. Pugh cringes as he swallows a mouthful of cold grey cottage pie.

MR. PUGH : *Pigs don't read at table, dear.*

Mrs. Pugh flicks the dust from the broken cruet. It rises and makes her cough.

MR. PUGH : *Pigs can't read, my dear.*

MRS. PUGH : *I know one who can.*

Mr. Pugh is now seen close, as he turns the pages of his book. There is a sound of another scream and we cut to a series of murders of ladies depicted in the old *Police Gazette*. The women are done in by gun, knife, hatchet, sea-water, and noose. Screams and shots sound.

FIRST VOICE : *Alone in the hissing laboratory of his wishes, Mr. Pugh minces among bad vats and jeroboams, tiptoes through spinneys of murdering herbs, agony dancing in his crucibles, and mixes especially for Mrs. Pugh a venomous porridge unknown to toxicologists which will scald and viper through her until her ears fall off like figs, her toes grow big and black as balloons, and steam comes screaming out of her navel.*

On a last close-up of a gunman with a moustache and a bowler-hat, cut on the noise of a shot back to Mr. Pugh as he nods, smiling, at the table.

MRS. PUGH'S VOICE : *Persons with manners . . .*

Now Mrs. Pugh is seen in her full steel across the table.

MRS. PUGH :*. . . Do not nod at table.*

Mr. Pugh cringes awake with soft-soaping smile under his long yellow moustache, worn in memory of Dr. Crippen.

MRS. PUGH : *You should wait until you retire to your* sty.

MR. PUGH smiling abjectly : *I beg your pardon, dear.*

He shovels some cottage pie into his mouth.

MR. PUGH : *You know best, my dear.*

MRS. PUGH : *What's that book by your trough, Mr. Pugh?*

MR. PUGH : *It's a theological work, my dear.* Lives of the Great Saints.

Mrs. Pugh is now seen in vicious close-up, smiling tight.

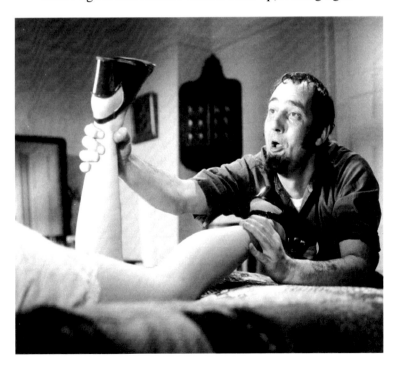

MRS. PUGH : *I saw a saint this morning. Saint Polly Garter. She was martyred again last night. Mrs. Organ Morgan . . .*

Now we are suddenly in the bright Organ Morgan dining-room, watching Mrs. Organ Morgan gabbling away as she shoves fish into her mouth.

Organ music sounds.

MRS. PUGH'S VOICE : *. . . Saw her with Mr. Waldo.*

MRS. ORGAN MORGAN : *And when they saw me they pretended they were looking for nests . . .*

Mrs. Organ Morgan fills her mouth with fish fuller than a pelican, but goes on talking.

MRS. ORGAN MORGAN : *But you don't go nesting in long com-binations, I said to myself, like Mr. Waldo was wearing, and your dress nearly over your head like Polly Garter's. Oh, they didn't fool me.*

With a huge gulp, Mrs. Organ Morgan swallows the fish in her mouth. We pull back to show that she is talking to Organ Morgan, who is sitting playing his portable organ.

MRS. ORGAN MORGAN : *And when you think of all those babies she's got, then all I can say is she'd better give up bird nesting that's all I can say, it isn't the right kind of hobby at all for a woman that can't say No even to midgets. Remember Bob Spit? He wasn't any bigger than a baby and he gave her two. But they're two nice boys, I will say that, Fred Spit and Arthur. Sometimes I like Fred best and sometimes I like Arthur. Who do you like best, Organ?*

Her husband turns round to grab a piece of bread with one hand, while he goes on playing the organ with the other.

ORGAN MORGAN : *Oh, Bach without any doubt. Bach every time for me.*

Now we move back quickly onto the wife.

MRS. ORGAN MORGAN : *Organ Morgan, you haven't been listening to a word I said. It's organ organ all the time with you. . .*

She bursts into tears, but at the same time, she nimbly spears some fish and swallows it in one gulp. Seen at the organ, her husband comments.

ORGAN MORGAN : *And then Palestrina.*

He shoves the hunk of bread into his mouth,, then turns back to his keyboard to play with both hands. Now we are in a

71

pigsty, where Bessie Bighead pours some swill in front of muddy noisy pigs.

FIRST VOICE : *Pigs grunt in a wet wallow-bath, and smile as they snort and dream . . .*

Now back in the hut on the headland, the First Voice rolls over to look at his watch. Beyond him, Norma Jane and the Second Voice lie listless. The First Voice pushes them to rise, and he sits up himself. Beyond him, the girl finds her trousers and begins to put them on, while the Second Voice goes for her jacket.

FIRST VOICE : . . . *They dream of the acorned swill of the world, the rooting for pig-fruit, the bag-pipe dugs of the mother sow, the squeal and snuffle of yesses of the women pigs in rut. They mud-bask and snout in the pig-loving sun; their tails curl; they rollick and slobber and snore to deep, smug, after-swill sleep.*

As Norma Jane kicks up her two legs to put on her trousers, we cut on the sound of ticking to :

The two hands on one of Lord Cut-Glass's clocks.

Lord Cut-Glass is now jerking from clock to chiming clock, checking their innards. In one hand, he carries a fish-head. He stops near us by a clock shaped like a ship's wheel, and we cut to

The ship's wheel on the railings inside Captain Cat's shore-bound cabin; beyond it, an old print of a whale and a ship. We move sideways to show Captain Cat slowly eating a single whitebait.

We can hear the sound of Polly Garter humming her song

. . . Back in the Welfare Hall, Polly Garter has finally finished scrubbing the whole wooden floor, which is sodden wet.

We begin a long pull back as she drops her brush and rag in her pail, stretches wearily, rises and picks up the pail, and walks away to a trestle table draped with the red dragon of Wales.

POLLY GARTER singing :

> *Now when farmers' boys on the first fair day*
> *Come down from the hills to drink and be gay*
> *Before the sun sinks I'll lie there in their arms*
> *For they're good bad boys from the lonely farms,*
> *But I always think as we tumble into bed*
> *Of little Willy Wee who is dead, dead . . .*

Now we see a long thin shelf of rock that sticks out into the sea below a cliff.

POLLY GARTER'S VOICE : . . . *Dead.*

We pan and tilt up the cliff side from the calm sea to show the outside of the hut on the headland.

FIRST VOICE : *The sea lolls, laps and idles in, with fishes sleeping in its lap.*

Out of the door of the hut comes the First Voice. He stands back as Norma Jane comes out and walks away up the path by the bullocks and goats, her scarf in her hand, not looking back. The Second Voice follows her out of the hut to stand by his master.

FIRST VOICE : *It all means nothing at all, and, howling for his milky mum, for her cawl and buttermilk and cowbreath and welshcakes . . .*

Now we see a medium close-up of the two Voices, looking sad and failed, as if what they had done had gone bad on them.

FIRST VOICE : . . . *And the fat birth-smelling bed and moonlit kitchen of her arms, he'll never forget as he paddles blind home through the weeping end of the world.*

On the quayside, we look through the window of the under-taker's shop to see Evans the Death loading a coffin into his hearse. He is wearing his purple gloves and is dressed in his full funeral clothes and pressing hard on his heart, which is jumping beneath his black suit.

EVANS THE DEATH : *Where's your dignity? Lie down.*

He bangs down the rear of the hearse to close it, and shatters the glass of the back window on the edge of the coffin.

Captain Cat's mittened fingers lovingly feel a walrus tooth, on which a whaling scene has been scratched in scrimshaw. We pull back, as music sounds, to show him with his memories in his cabin in Schooner House.

SECOND VOICE : *Captain Cat, at his window thrown wide to the sun and the clippered seas he sailed long ago . . .*

In a dive bar, the young Captain Cat stands, his eyes large and blue, his beard black, a gold ring in his ear. By his side, a lout. The lout picks a fight, the young Cat throws beer in his face, the lout pulls a knife, the young Cat breaks a bottle as a weapon, then kicks the lout down through a bar screen.

All of Cat's dreams are gauzed with memory.

SECOND VOICE : . . . *When his eyes were blue and bright, slumbers and voyages; ear-ringed and rolling, I Love You Rosie Probert tattooed on his belly, he brawls with broken bottles in the fug and babel of the dark dock bars . . .*

Now the young Cat leans over the bar to kiss a henna-red barmaid, while his hand gropes at the breasts of a cuffing mulatress.

SECOND VOICE : . . . *Roves with a herd of short and good time cows in every naughty port and twines and souses with the drowned and blowzy-breasted dead.*

Now we are in Rosie Probert's bedroom, where she sits on her quilt on her brass bed, looking up with her eyes like moons.

Rosie turns towards the bedhead, stretching an arm.

ROSIE PROBERT : *Tom Cat . . . Tom Cat . . .*

SECOND VOICE : *One voice of all he remembers most dearly as his dream buckets down. Lazy early Rosie . . .*

We move across to the bedhead, where the young Cat is climbing over the brass rail, pulling off his sea-boots as he comes.

He falls into the laughing arms of Rosie.

SECOND VOICE : *In that gulf and haven, fleets by the dozen have anchored for the little heaven of the night . . .*

Now we are outside Rosie's Cottage by the sea. Ducks quack at the queue of sailors outside her door. Tom-Fred the donkey-man, one of the Drowned Dead from Captain Cat's first dream, comes out of the door, doing up his trousers. He nods and winks at the sailor first in the queue, who is the one who sang *Santiana.*

ROSIE PROBERT'S VOICE : *Quack twice and ask for Rosie, Jack.*

TOM-FRED : *Bloody good value.*

SINGING SAILOR : *Hey Tom, lend us a dollar . . .*

Tom-Fred walks off and the other sailor goes in to Rosie. Back in his cabin at Schooner House, the old Cat's eyes fill as he remembers . . .

SECOND VOICE : *But she speaks to Captain napping Cat alone. Rosie Probert is the one love of his sea-life that was sardined with women.*

Now we move in on the haunting eyes of Rosie Probert sitting on her brass bed. Music sounds softly.

ROSIE PROBERT'S VOICE

> *What seas did you see,*
> *Tom Cat, Tom Cat,*
> *In your sailoring days*
> *Long long ago?*
> *What sea beasts were . . .*

The old Captain is now seen from beneath, sitting in his high wooden chair.

ROSIE PROBERT'S VOICE :

> *. . . In the wavery green*
> *When you were my master?*

CAPTAIN CAT : *I'll tell you the truth . . .*

Now we see an old seal lying on pebbles in the sea spume.

CAPTAIN CAT'S VOICE :

> *. . . Seas barking like seals*
> *Blue seas and green . . .*

Back in the Cabin, the old Cat speaks his memories.

CAPTAIN CAT :

> *. . . Seas covered with eels*
> *And mermen and whales.*

ROSIE PROBERT'S VOICE :

> *What seas did you sail*
> *Old whaler when . . .*

In three quick shots, we see the grizzled Cat throw a harpoon from a whale-boat at a whale in the spray, then hunch back to take the strain on the rope.

ROSIE PROBERT'S VOICE :

> *. . . On the blubbery waves*
> *Between Frisco and Wales*
> *You were my bosun?*

Young and smiling and eyeing over the cheroot in his mouth, the young Cat stands at Rosie's brass bed-rail.

CAPTAIN CAT'S VOICE :

> *As true as I'm here*
> *Dear you Tom Cat's tart . . .*

Now we move slowly in to hold the violet-deep eyes of Rosie Probert.

CAPTAIN CAT'S VOICE :
>... *You landlubber Rosie*
>*You cosy love*
>*My easy as easy*
>*My true sweetheart* ...

We move up the brass rail at the end of Rosie's bed to show her between the sheets with the young Cat, a dark bottle of rum between them. Cat pulls up his vest to show laughing Rosie her name tattooed on his belly, then they fall to kissing.

CAPTAIN CAT'S VOICE :

> *. . . Seas green as a bean*
> *Seas gliding with swans*
> *In the seal-barking moon.*

ROSIE PROBERT'S VOICE :

> *What seas were rocking*
> *My little deck hand*
> *My favourite husband*
> *In your seaboots and hunger*
> *My duck my whaler . . .*

Suddenly Rosie is seen rolling in the hot arms of Tom-Fred the donkeyman.

ROSIE PROBERT'S VOICE :

> *. . . My honey my daddy*
> *My pretty sugar sailor*
> *With my name on your belly . . .*

Now she rolls again in the hug of the young Cat.

ROSIE PROBERT'S VOICE :

> *. . . When you were a boy*
> *Long long ago?*

Now the old Cat is seen back in his cabin, talking to the past and the lost.

CAPTAIN CAT :

> *I'll tell you no lies.*
> *The only sea I saw . . .*

Now Rosie moans in silent joy or pain on her pillows, dying of joy or sickness. We pan off her face onto the brass bedhead and the wall.

CAPTAIN CAT'S VOICE :

> *. . . Was the seesaw sea*
> *With you riding on it.*
> *Lie down, lie easy*
> *Let me shipwreck in your thighs.*

Two black-gloved hands pick up from a rosy plate two pennies with an old dead king's head on them. The hands put the pennies on the eyes of Rosie Probert, lying stretched out on a table.

We slowly pull back to show her body laid out with candles burning beyond.

ROSIE PROBERT'S VOICE :
> *Knock twice, Jack*
> *At the door of my grave*
> *And ask for Rosie.*

CAPTAIN CAT'S VOICE :
> *Rosie Probert.*

ROSIE PROBERT'S VOICE :
> *Remember her.*
> *She is forgetting.*
> *The earth which filled her mouth*
> *Is vanishing from her.*
> *Remember me.*
> *I have forgotten you.*
> *I am going into the darkness*
> *   of the darkness for ever .. .*

A young seal waits on the edge of the breakers. We move in on its lying shape.

ROSIE PROBERT'S VOICE :
> *. . . I have forgotten that I was ever born . . .*

The old Captain weeps at his window, crying out.

CAPTAIN CAT : *Come back! Come back!*

We drop down outside his window to where Gwennie and her mother are walking along the sunny quayside.

CAPTAIN CAT'S VOICE : *Come back! Come back!*

Gwennie looks up at Cat in his window in Schooner House.

GWENNIE : *Look, Captain Cat is crying. He's crying all over his nose. He's got a nose like strawberries.*

Mother and daughter move down Cockle Row.

Now we see, between the backs of Gwennie and her mother, Nogood Boyo lying in his boat attached by a rope to the dockside. He is fishing with his toes.

GWENNIE : *Nogood Boyo gave me three pennies yesterday but I wouldn't.*

NOGOOD BOYO calling up : *Hello, Gwennie. I'll give you six pennies.*

On Gwennie's giggle, Nogood lies back in his boat.

On a sea headland of grass and yellow gorse, Mae Rose Cottage sits among her goats, pulling at the petals of a flower.

MAE ROSE COTTAGE :

He loves me, he loves me not

He loves me, he loves me not . . .

In his dinghy, the *Zanzibar,* Nogood Boyo lies on his back, dreaming, a fishing line tied to his foot. There is a sudden tug on the line. Nogood bends his leg until he can get a hand on the line to pull it in. At the end of the line is a corset.

NOGOOD BOYO : *Bloody funny fish!*

He puts the corset down in the boat as his pillow, and lies back in a day-dream. Skiffle music sounds. Out of the waves emerges Mrs. Dai Bread Two, wearing only a bangle on her wrist. She stretches up her arms and her breasts.

In the Zanzibar, Nogood holds out the dripping corset.

NOGOOD BOYO : *Would you like this nice wet corset, Mrs. Dai Bread Two?*

Now in Nogood's dream again, the hard and laughing Mrs. Dai Bread Two is covered with shining scales of armour, while Nogood himself wades into the sea, offering her the corset.

NOGOOD BOYO : *Would you like this nice corset, Mrs. Dai Bread . . .*

MRS. DAI BREAD TWO : *No, I won't!*

NOGOOD BOYO : *And a bite of my apple?*

Screaming with glee, Mrs. Dai Bread Two pulls Nogood down into her cold and scaly embrace, as the camera and the music tilt up and swell to show the two in a great sweep of bay and sea.

Back in the dinghy, Nogood's eyes close, his hands move towards his belly. He twitches in his sleep, dreaming . . . As Lily Smalls scrubs in the wash-house, Nogood steals up behind her with his wet corset. She takes it from him and tries it on, while he lifts up her skirt from behind.

LILY SMALLS : *Oh, you're up to no good, Boyo . . .*

She struggles lovingly in his hug.

Back in the *Zanzibar,* Nogood wakes out of his sleep and looks up reproachfully at the sky.

NOGOOD BOYO : *I want to be a good boyo, but nobody'll let me.*

Mae Rose Cottage is lying back on the headland, pulling the last petal off the flower. Her thighs are spread open towards camera under her dress.

MAE ROSE COTTAGE : *He* loves *me! - the dirty old fool.*

Mae Rose Cottage lies back dreamily on the sunny grass and stretches and yearns, with her white nanny-goats by her.

SECOND VOICE : *Seventeen and never been sweet in the grass ho ho . . .*

Now we see sheep pouring over a bank and through a gap in a hedge round a pasture.

SECOND VOICE : *High above in Salt Lake Farm Mr. Utah Watkins naps and counts the wife-faced sheep . . .*

UTAH WATKINS VOICE : *Thirty-four, thirty-five . . .*

Now we cut to the farmhouse kitchen, where Utah Watkins lies snoozing and counting sheep by the fire.

UTAH WATKINS : *Thirty-six, forty-eight, eighty-nine . . .*

The sheep keep on pouring over the bank.

MRS. UTAH WATKINS VOICE :

> *Knit one slip one*
> *Knit two together . . .*

Now we see Mrs. Utah Watkins in her chair by the fire, as she knits an enormous scarf, full of holes. Her cat walks over the endless wool comforter.

MRS. UTAH WATKINS :

> *Pass the slipstitch over*
> *Knit one slip one . . .*

In Bethesda graveyard, the Reverend Eli Jenkins stands praying by an ornate overgrown tombstone marked *The Reverend Daffyd Jenkins, May He Rest In Peace.*

MRS. UTAH WATKINS VOICE :

> *Knit two together . . .*

REVEREND ELI JENKINS : *Poor Dad . . . to die of drink and agriculture.*

As he walks away from his father's grave, we cut to . . . An old man, Eli's father, lying asleep with his whisky bottle, amid the sunny yellow gorse. Above him, a labourer sickles through the yellow and orange thorny bushes. He swings his sickle down, mouths 'Christ' on a scream, and a branch of orange flowers falls into camera.

Now we are under the green hat of Llaregyb Hill, as a herd of cows moves and moos slowly towards us, on their way to milking.

FIRST VOICE : *The meadows still as Sunday . . .*

In Milk Wood, the two Voices walk downhill back towards the town. The cows' noise tells them that they are near Salt Lake Farm.

FIRST VOICE : . . . *The shut-eye tasselled bulls, the goat-and daisy dingles, nap happy and lazy . . .*

Higher up the hill, a white mare and her foal graze. Clouds top the crest of the mild green slope, and the wind takes them away.

FIRST VOICE : . . . *The dumb duck-ponds snooze. Clouds sag and pillow on Llaregyb Hill.*

In the farmyard of Salt Lake Farm, Utah Watkins curses his cattle driving them in for milking.

UTAH WATKINS : *Ho, ho! Ho, ho! Damn you, you damned dairies!*

Smiling, the huge Bessie Bighead guides the cows gently off, calling each by name.

BESSIE BIGHEAD :

> *Peg, Meg, Buttercup, Moll,*
> *Fan from the Castle,*
> *Theodosia and Daisy.*

Utah Watkins furiously beats his herding-stick on the ground.

UTAH WATKINS : *I'll have you for chops, mince pies, bone soup! But where'll I get my bloody milk then?*

Now we see Bessie Bighead again pouring swill to the pigs in the farmyard, while a gross farmhand, Gomer Owen, steals up behind her, plants a kiss on her cheek and runs away.

FIRST VOICE : *Bessie Bighead, conceived in Milk Wood, born in a barn, wrapped in paper, left on a doorstep, big-headed and bass-voiced . . .*

In medium close-up, we see Bessie slowly smile, as Gomer runs away.

FIRST VOICE : . . . *She grew in the dark until long-dead Gomer Owen kissed her when she wasn't looking because he was dared.*

BESSIE BIGHEAD'S VOICE : *Alone till I die.*

In a cowstall now, with her milk-pail and stool, Bessie comes to a cow, sits and begins to milk it expertly, her head thrust against its flank.

FIRST VOICE : *Now in the light she'll work, sing, milk, say the cows' sweet names and sleep until the night sucks out her soul and spits it into the sky. In her life-long love light, holily Bessie milks the fond lake-eyed cows . . .*

In close-up, we see Bessie's hand squirting milk from the cow's udder.

FIRST VOICE : . . . *As dusk showers slowly down over byre, sea and town.*

In the farmyard, Utah Watkins pulls at the halter on a placid cow, and talks down to his dog.

UTAH WATKINS : *Bite her to death!*

The dog slinks away, so the disgusted farmer looks up at the contented cow.

UTAH WATKINS : *Gore him, sit on him, Daisy.*

The cow backs off.

There is an outbreak of bullocks bellowing outside the farm wall, as the Second Voice skids on the tail of a bullock down the hill. The First Voice turns away from the farmyard wall, laughing. The Second Voice still rides the bullock's tail.

The First Voice walks down to join his jester, who shoos away the bullock. Then both Voices walk away by the farm-yard wall.

In the farm by the stables, Utah Watkins, mounted on a great carthorse, thumps and wallops it as it stands still.

UTAH WATKINS : *Gallop, you bleeding cripple! Gallop, you bleeding cripple!*

The horse neighs with laughter, and moves backwards. Now we are in the overgrown graveyard in the last light of the sun, as Norma Jane walks towards us, and disappears in darkness under a yew tree by camera.

FIRST VOICE : *Now the town is dusk. Each cobble, donkey, goose and gooseberry street is a thoroughfare of dusk; and dusk . . .*

The two men now walk down the hill from the farm towards the town lying below about the harbour. Move with them as we see the first lamplight burning . . .

FIRST VOICE : . . . *And ceremonial dust, and night's first darkening snow, and the sleep of birds, drift under and through the live dusk of this place of love. Llaregyb is the capital of dusk.*

We close on a white clouded roof, then cut to . . .

The blind on Mrs. Ogmore-Pritchard's window as she closes it with a snap and sits on her high-backed chair by her bed.

With a pop of her lips she summons her dead husbands inside.

MRS. OGMORE-PRITCHARD : *Husbands!*

Seen from the porch of the house, Mr. Ogmore and Mr. Pritchard try to go in last, as they walk up the front garden from the quayside.

MR. PRITCHARD : *You first, Mr. Ogmore.*

MR. OGMORE : *After you, Mr. Pritchard.*

MR. PRITCHARD : *You first, Mr. Ogmore.*

MR. OGMORE : *After you, Mr. Pritchard.*

MR. PRITCHARD : *No, no, Mr. Ogmore. You widowed her first.*

The two ghosts of the dead husbands vanish as they collide and stick in the porch entrance. As Mrs. Ogmore-Pritchard sits alone on her bed, looking to her front, her two dead husbands are suddenly on either side of her, also looking to their fronts.

MRS. OGMORE-PRITCHARD : *I love you* both.

MR. OGMORE : *Oh, Mrs. Ogmore.*

MR. PRITCHARD : *Oh, Mrs. Pritchard.*

MRS. OGMORE-PRITCHARD : *Soon it will be time to go to bed. Tell me your tasks in order.*

MR. OGMORE and MR. PRITCHARD : *We must take our pyjamas from the drawer marked pyjamas.*

MRS. OGMORE-PRITCHARD : *And then you must take them off.*

Her ghost husbands look at each other in horror.

On the sea headland in the evening, Mae Rose Cottage has undone her blouse and is drawing circles of lipstick round her nipples.

Beyond her, a bearded nannygoat champs and sneers. Mae Rose Cottage goes on drawing scarlet circles round her nipples.

MAE ROSE COTTAGE : *I'm fast I'm a bad lot. God will strike me dead. I'm seventeen. I'll go to hell.*

The small white kid passes her, flicking its ears, not caring. She pushes out her breasts with her hands to make them bigger.

MAE ROSE COTTAGE : *You just wait. I'll sin till I blow up!*

She turns round to the sneering nannygoat.

MAE ROSE COTTAGE : *Oh you go home!*

Outside Bethesda House, the Reverend Eli Jenkins appears to recite his sunset poem. There is the sound of organ music.

ELI JENKINS :

> *Every morning when I wake*
> *Dear Lord, a little prayer I make,*
> *O please to keep Thy lovely eye*
> *On all poor creatures born to die.*
> *And every evening at sun-down . . .*

Now we see that the light on his face is coming from the low sun beyond a rookery, where the dark birds fly and caw.

ELI JENKINS VOICE :

> *. . . I ask a blessing on the town,*
> *For whether we last the night or no*
> *I'm sure is always touch-and-go.*

In the shadow of the dusk, Mae Rose Cottage pulls her goats up the hill on their way home.

Below her, the whole long length of the evening town, as it lounges out into the bay.

ELI JENKINS VOICE :

> *We are not wholly bad or good*
> *Who live our lives under Milk Wood . . .*

The very last of the sun disappears behind rayed clouds, mystical and bright.

ELI JENKINS VOICE :
> *. . . And Thou, I know, wilt be the first*
> *To see our best side . . .*

Suddenly, we are back in the overgrown graveyard by the black yew-tree and the forbidding church. Mae Rose Cottage and Gossamer Beynon stand talking by the goats. Coming up behind them is Jack Black, the persecuting Bible-mad cobbler, with his lantern and holy book at the ready to scour out sin.

ELI JENKINS VOICE : *. . . Not our worst.*

JACK BLACK : *There is Satan in Milk Wood! Off to Gomorrah! Off to Gomorrah! Ach y fi! Ach y fi!*

He pursues the screaming girls and the goats up the steep slope of the dark wood, where the black-handed branches come gripping down.

In their lovely sloppy room, Cherry Owen kisses Mrs. Cherry good-bye.

CHERRY OWEN : *I always say she's got two husbands, one drunk and one sober.*

MRS. CHERRY OWEN : *And aren't I a lucky woman? Because I love them both.*

She looks radiant after him, as he goes off to booze in the pub.

The Sailor's Arms is very quiet, as Cherry Owen enters to see Sinbad there with the two Fishermen, still drinking silently, and Mr. Waldo, now very tipsy.

SINBAD SAILORS : *Evening, Cherry.*

CHERRY OWEN : *Evening, Sinbad.*

SINBAD SAILORS : *What'll you have?*

CHERRY OWEN : *Too much.*

SINBAD SAILORS : *The Sailors' Arms is always open . .*

We move in on him as he pulls at the beerpump.

SINBAD : *Oh, Gossamer, open yours!*

Under the dark branches, through the dark trees of Milk Wood, the two men come walking, the First Voice striding to the front.

FIRST VOICE : *Dusk is drowned for ever until tomorrow. It is all at once night now . . .*

Now we see the two men walking down through the dark wood into the overgrown graveyard, where the Second Voice trips and sprawls over a tomb.

FIRST VOICE : . . . *The windy town is a hill of windows, and from the larrupped waves the lights of the lamps in the windows call back the day and the dead that have run away to sea . . .*

In Polly Garter's hovel, we start on a bed full of children and a dog, then move to Polly as she turns away with a baby in her arms and puts it to sleep in an old wash-tub.

FIRST VOICE : . . . *All over the calling dark, babies and old men are bribed and lullabied to sleep.*

POLLY GARTER singing :

> *Rockabye, grandpa, in the tree top,*
> *When the wind blows the cradle will rock,*
> *When the bough breaks the cradle will fall,*
> *Down will come grandpa, whiskers and all.*

She has moved across to where her old Grandfather sits by the stove, swaddled in a blanket. She uses the leg of his chair to put on one of her garters with roses.

POLLY GARTER : *Sleep you.*

POLLY'S GRANDFATHER : *I won't.*

POLLY GARTER : *It'll be morning soon.*

She puts on her shawl.

POLLY'S GRANDFATHER : *Suppose I'm not here to see it?*

Polly bends and kisses the old man and leaves.

POLLY'S GRANDFATHER : *Who are you seeing? You'll be getting more babies.*

Inside Bethesda chapel, Organ Morgan sits playing the organ, while the Reverend Eli Jenkins smiles his content and walks towards the chapel door. On the bar of the Sailor's Arms, seventeen empty pint mugs stand in front of Cherry Owen and Mr. Waldo, as they drink in rhythm to the sound of the distant organ music.

MR. WALDO : *Down with the waltzing and the skipping.*

CHERRY OWEN : *Dancing isn't natural.*

Cherry downs another pint.

In her bedroom, Mae Rose Cottage dances from one mirror to another in her transparent petticoat. On her face is a haughty

look, then a melting one, as the organ music plays. She breathes to her reflection in the glass.

MAE ROSE COTTAGE : *Oh, come and get me, Mister Anybody.*

Back in the Sailor's Arms, both Cherry and Mr. Waldo lift up another pint and begin their swaying motion before lowering the ale.

CHERRY OWEN : *Oh, boyo . . .*

In the overgrown graveyard, the Second Voice has fallen on a tombstone. The First Voice helps him to his feet. They hear the noise of the chapel door opening, and they move away.

The Reverend Eli Jenkins comes out of Bethesda chapel, and walks down the path in front of it, looking round at the night trees.

ELI JENKINS : *Milk Wood on the hill, the memorial of peoples that dwelt in the region of Llaregyb before the Celts left the Land of Summer and where the old wizards made themselves . . .*

The Reverend Jenkins catches sight of someone in the wood, and we see . . .

Polly Garter walking through the snowdrops and the trees.

ELI JENKINS VOICE : *. . . A wife out of flowers.*

In the bar of the Sailor's Arms, where there are about a dozen drinkers now, two men play dominos.

An accordion-player strikes up a tune and Mr. Waldo does a song-and-dance act, light and slow with fat grace. As he dances, the camera moves from side to side behind the domino players to show the rest of the people in the bar egging on Waldo.

MR. WALDO singing :

> *In Pembroke City when I was young*
> *I lived by the Castle Keep*
> *Sixpence a week was my wages*
> *For working for the chimbley sweep.*
> *Six cold pennies he gave me*
> *Not a farthing more or less . . .*

We are closer now on Waldo as he puffs and rises and falls.

MR. WALDO :

> *And all the fare I could afford*
> *Was parsnip gin and watercress . . .*

Now we are in the wood, as Polly Garter lies down on her shawl on a mossy tree-stump, bright with flowers.

MR. WALDO'S VOICE :

> *. . . I did not need a knife and fork*
> *Or a bib up to my chin . . .*

Again we move from side to side, watching Waldo's dance and the others joining in. Sinbad even pours beer into Waldo's bowler, which Waldo tips into his mug.

MR. WALDO :

> *. . . To dine on a dish of watercress*
> *And a jug of parsnip gin.*
> *Did you ever hear a growing boy*
> *To live so cruel cheap*
> *On grub that has no flesh and bones*
> *And liquor that makes you weep?*
> *Sweep sweep chimbley sweep,*
> *I wept through Pembroke City*
> *Poor and barefoot in the snow*
> *Till a kind young woman took pity.*
> *Poor little chimbley sweep she said*
> *Black as the ace of spades*

O nobody's swept my chimbley
Since my husband went his ways . . .

Now Waldo gets all the people in the pub to join in the chorus of his song.

MR. WALDO AND VOICES :

Come and sweep my chimbley
Come and sweep my chimbley . . .

Seen in close-up Polly Garter finds a black beetle crawling on her dress, picks it up, and puts it aside. She stares sadly above her at nothing.

MR. WALDO AND VOICES :

. . . She sighed to me with a blush
Come and sweep my chimbley
Come and sweep my chimbley . . .

In the Sailor's Arms, Waldo lurches to the end of his dance.

MR. WALDO AND VOICES :

Bring along your chimbley brush!

Waldo ends his dance by falling flat on his back on the floor. He roars with laughter as he lies in the dust.

Cherry Owen is seen from below as he tips his beer mug down.

Seen from above, Waldo's face is spattered with beer.

Now we see the froth from Cherry Owen's mug pouring all over the screen with his laughing face above and we dissolve to . . .

Captain Cat still sitting in his chair as the tears roll down his face.

CAPTAIN CAT : *Dancing Williams!*

FIRST DROWNED'S VOICE : *Still dancing.*

Three of the drowned sailors seem to dance a hornpipe round the grey-gauzed Rosie Probert . . . who runs in her beauty towards camera and is gone.

ROSIE PROBERT'S VOICE : *Rosie, with God. She has forgotten dying.*

In the graveyard, the Second Voice peers over the top of Rosie Probert's tombstone, while the First Voice stands nearby against a tree.

SECOND VOICE : *Listen to the night breaking.*

The Second Voice crawls forward, leaving the First Voice by the tree.

FIRST VOICE : *The dead come out in their Sunday best.*

Out of the chapel, Organ Morgan comes. He sees Mr. Waldo hurrying away from a lying bearded shape on a tomb. He approaches, and sees the vision he is looking for.

ORGAN MORGAN : *Johann Sebastian!*

Cherry Owen looks up from the tombstone, drunkenly.

CHERRY OWEN : *Who?*

ORGAN MORGAN : *Johann Sebastian mighty Bach. Oh, Bach fach.*

CHERRY OWEN : *To hell with you.*

He lies back on the tombstone, and closes his eyes.

In his dream, Cherry Owen sees himself sitting in a pew in the pub. A fish-head sticks out of his pint mug. He drinks deeply and swallows the fish down whole.

In her bedroom, neat and tidy and prim and happy, Myfanwy Price strokes her own self through her knitted bedjacket covered with hearts and patterns.MYFANWY PRICE : *Oh, my Mog, I am yours for ever.*

In his emporium, Mog Edwards beams, five-pound notes and coins falling from his straw hat.

MOG EDWARDS VOICE : *Come to my arms, Myfanwy.*

Now the drunk Mr Waldo lies on Polly Garter, who looks up at the trees sadly.

Track up from her rosy garters across to the dark Milk Wood.

POLLY GARTER'S VOICE :

But I always think as we tumble into bed
Of little Willy Wee . . .

Now we move across from where the Second Voice is kneeling and nuzzling the gravestone of Norma Jane Jenkins.

POLLY GARTER'S VOICE :

. . . Who is dead, dead, dead.

We move on to where the First Voice is standing in the night wood by the gravestones.

FIRST VOICE :

Now behind the eyes and the secrets
Of the dreamers in the streets
Rocked to sleep by the sea
See the . . .

As he turns and walks away into the wood, we cut on the noise of a pig squealing to . . .

The Second Voice who, like a medieval devil, rides a great boar down Coronation Street. It squeals as he leaps off. Two

black horses paw and run frightened around their high field on the edge of the world.

The First Voice, a black shape against black trees, conjures up the spells of darkness.

Strange music sounds, wild cries and the noise of seals moaning among the breakers.

Leaping away from the boar, the Second Voice leads the night-clothed people of Llaregyb in a wild dream dance clockwise and widdershins round the town pump, where P.C. Attila Rees sits in his nightshirt, conducting the dance with his truncheon.

Mr. Waldo knocks off his helmet and dances by with Polly Garter.

The Neighbour women cavort and float into the dream dance from their cottage doorways. Willy Nilly bounces by.

Organ Morgan leaps, rude and ginger.

P.C. Rees conducts from the pump.

Dai Bread balloons on his round, with his wives spinning after him.

Mr. Waldo pulls along the laughing Polly Garter.

Gossamer Beynon drifts in joy, fair hair abandoned.

Willy Nilly laughs loose on his whirligigs.

The Second Voice crouches and soars, scooping the swoop of the dance at his circling heels.

Now P.C. Rees rises on the pump, and dances off.

Organ Morgan leaps wild and mad and away after. . .

… Lord Cut-Glass and the rest of the dreaming dancers as the Second Voice leads the ring of people in a line down Coronation Street from the square towards the sea. In the harbour now, a dozen of the people dance after the Second Voice down the shelving shore towards the sea. Their wild cries become the shrieking of gulls. The Second Voice conducts them from the side as they dance past him towards the whispering water, then dissolve into . .

… Seals, that slide and moan and hump away into the white foam, the Celtic myth shapes of the drowned dead and the bodies of the dreamers run away to sea . . . Now we dissolve back to the harbour shore, where the Second Voice is still conducting the dream dance with great swoops of his arms. He is alone on the strand now. His hands drop to his sides, the music dies, and he turns and walks back up the slope. The sea is calm behind him.

FIRST VOICE : *The thin night darkens. The breeze from the creased water sighs the streets close . . .*

In the dark wood, the First Voice smiles secretly, seems to cross himself, and moves off.

FIRST VOICE : *. . . Under Milk waking Wood. The Wood, whose every tree-foot's cloven ...*

Now on the crest of the hill under the dark trees of the wood, we see the black shapes of the First and Second Voices going away from the town up the crest into the night for ever.

FIRST VOICE :*. . . In the black glad sight of the hunters of lovers, that is a God-built garden to Mary Ann Sailors who knows there is Heaven on earth and the chosen people of His kind fire in Llaregyb's land, that is the fairday farmhands' wantoning ignorant chapel of bridesbeds, and, to the Reverend Eli Jenkins, a greenleaved sermon on the innocence of men . . .*

Again we track forwards under the dark branches of the wood that grope towards us and make crooked fingers against the moony dark.

FIRST VOICE : . . . *The suddenly wind-shaken wood springs*
awake for second dark time this one Spring day.

A clear woman's voice sings a Welsh lullaby over the END
CREDITS, which appear on the branches of Milk Wood as
they thin away into the night sky.

Andrew Sinclair with Richard Burton

David Jason with Ruth Madoc

Boy Dylan at Fern Hill

Mumbles Pier

Aeronwy Thomas at the
Boathouse in Laugharne

Mid Dylan by the docks
and slag-heaps of
Swansea

Dylan Thomas at
The White Horse Tavern

Mid Dylan at the grave of Dylan Thomas

"UNDER MILK WOOD is a classic! I have seen the film three times; I shall see it at least three times more. Pure poetry!"
—JUDITH CRIST, New York Magazine

"UNDER MILK WOOD seems like a miracle and a lovely one at that...perfect and unique!"
—BERNARD DREW, Gannett News Service

"UNDER MILK WOOD is a glowingly beautiful film! Be sure—be absolutely sure—to see it!"
—GENE SHALIT, Ladies Home Journal

"UNDER MILK WOOD is a beautiful, heady mixture of poetry and visual art. A concert for the eyes!"
—LOUISE SWEENEY, Christian Science Monitor

"UNDER MILK WOOD is an accomplishment of considerable magnitude. O'Toole and Burton are almost awesomely fine."
—NORMA McLAIN STOOP, After Dark

"UNDER MILK WOOD is a fascinating piece of work...lovely and dream like, a tone-poem of powerful moods and emotions."
—BOB SALMAGGI, Group W Network

"UNDER MILK WOOD has an incandescent poetic intelligence that gleams through every line."
—BRUCE WILLIAMSON, Playboy

JULES BUCK & HUGH FRENCH present AN ANDREW SINCLAIR FILM

RICHARD BURTON
ELIZABETH TAYLOR
PETER O'TOOLE

in DYLAN THOMAS'

UNDER MILK WOOD

SCREENPLAY AND DIRECTION ANDREW SINCLAIR GUEST STARS GLYNIS JOHNS · VIVIEN MERCHANT · SIAN PHILLIPS · EXECUTIVE PRODUCERS JULES BUCK · HUGH FRENCH
MUSIC COMPOSED BY BRIAN GASCOIGNE · ASSOCIATE PRODUCER JOHN COMFORT · A TIMON FILMS PRODUCTION · COLOR BY TECHNICOLOR · DISTRIBUTED BY ALTURA FILMS INTERNATIONAL [PG]

Andrew Sinclair

Andrew Sinclair is a leading novelist, historian and film-maker. He did his graduate work at Harvard and Columbia University, then he taught at Cambridge and London University in England. He is an experienced lecturer on History, English Literature and the Cinema with a particular knowledge of Dylan Thomas. Not only did he write the recent biography of Dylan and direct the film of Under Milk Wood, but he has also adapted for the stage Dylan's novel "Adventures in the Skin Trade".

DYLAN ON DYLAN

Written and Directed

after DYLAN THOMAS

by

Andrew Sinclair

Timon Films

Published by Timon Films
Flat 20, Millennium House,
132 Grosvenor Road, London SW1V 3JY

Time Out gave this exceptional documentary taken from the words of the poet
Dylan Thomas a 4**** (four star) rating. And of Sinclair's biography *Dylan
the Bard*, *The Times* stated:

SINCLAIR, WHO made the classic film of the Dylan Thomas play *Under
Milk Wood*, has updated his 1975 biography of Thomas with excellent results.
Thomas's life was an odd blend of gregariousness and solitude, with hours
spent drinking away his erratic earnings in pubs dotted around London and
Wales.

Sinclair conveys in words and photographs the poet's cherubic features
and mop of golden hair. He brings Thomas's appealing physical appearance to
life and conveys sympathetically his tempestuous marriage to Caitlin
McNamara.

The poet's life in the Thirties reads like a "who's who" of Fitzrovia and
Bloomsbury. His drinking companions included characters such as Nina
Hamnett, John Lehman, Djuna Barnes and, later, the Sitwells. Sinclair's
writing is quirky, presenting unique turns of phrase which are unlikely to be
seen elsewhere: "Whatever he boasted, however much Dylan seemed a tiddler
in the London depths, or indeed a chicken in a country Eden" is one such
example. For this reason the book is an unpredictable but entertaining romp
through a life.

Sinclair succeeds in his aim to reveal the "real" Dylan Thomas with his
affectionate, colourful portrait of his subject.

Vanessa Curtis

DYLAN ON DYLAN

CAST

STARRING

RICHARD BURTON	*First Voice*
PETER O'TOOLE	*Captain Cat*
ELIZABETH TAYLOR	*Rosie Probert*
DAVID HEMMINGS	*Young Dylan*
DAVID JASON	*Nogood Boyo*

with

ANGHARAD REES]	
AERONWY THOMAS]	*Caitlin MacNamara*
VINCENT PENFOLD	*Mid Dylan*
BOB KINGDOM	*Old Dylan*
RYAN DAVIES	*Second Voice*
RUTH MADOC	*Mrs Dai Bread Two*
SUSAN PENHALIGON	*Mae Rose Cottage*
AUBREY RICHARDS	*Reverend Eli Jenkins*
ROBERT EDDISON	*Mr D.J. Thomas*
BARBARA KEOGH	*Mrs Florence Thomas*
BRIDGET TURNER	*Nancy Thomas*

CAMERA AND EDITING	*Julian Gibsone*
FIRST ASSISTANT	*Jim Watson*

As the Welsh producer, we are most grateful to JEFF TOWNS for his expertise in DYLAN THOMAS material and location finding, also to PAUL DAVIES of the Volcano Theatre Company for his help in casting the roles of BOY DYLAN, the BARMAID and the PUB CUSTOMER, the PASSER-BY and the HUNCHBACK IN THE PARK, and the PARK-KEEPER.

PERMISSIONS

We are most grateful for permissions granted by and for the copyright holders in the film of DYLAN ON DYLAN.

THE IMPERIAL WAR MUSEUM and ARCHIVE

Extracts from: Wales/Green Mountain, Black Mountain
                               Balloon Site 568
                               A City Reborn (Coventry)
                               These are the Men

THE BOURNVILLE VILLAGE TRUST

Extracts from: When We Build Again

DAVID HIGHAM ASSOCIATES *for the* DYLAN THOMAS ESTATE

Extracts from:

FILM SCRIPT: Under Milk Wood

NOVEL
(adapted as play & film):   Adventures in the Skin Trade
                               Portrait of the Artist as a Young Dog
                                    'Just Like Little Dogs'

RADIO SCRIPTS: Return Journey
                               A Visit to America

LETTERS (to Daniel Jones)

POEMS: Now I was Young and Easy …
                               The Hunchback in the Park
                               In My Craft and Sullen Art …
                               Poem in October
                               And Death Shall Have No Dominion
                               Lament
                               Do Not Go Gentle Into That Good Night …
                               Prologue
                               Fern Hill

DYLAN ON DYLAN

The OPENING CREDITS are played over an approach from the sea towards the boathouse at Laugharne. We hear OLWEN REES singing a Welsh folksong.

We CUT to an extract from 'WALES – GREEN MOUNTAIN, BLACK MOUNTAIN', a war documentary which was written by DYLAN THOMAS.

COMMENTATOR (V.O.): *Wales is a mountain of strength. The valleys grew rich, but all the time the power and wealth of the world were rocking, rocking. ...*

Unemployed miners take coal from slagheaps

MID DYLAN (V.O.): *In 1914, when the First World War began, a baby was born.*

The infant DYLAN THOMAS is seen in his mother's lap.

MID DYLAN (V.O.): *Dylan - it means a son of the wave – was an angel child in his mother's lap –*

A photographic portrait of the seated D.J. THOMAS slowly FADES INTO the bearded powerful top-hatted face of his great-uncle, GWILYM.

MID DYLAN (V.O.): *Here she sits with her mother beside his father D.J. Thomas, a schoolteacher in Swansea in Wales. His great-uncle Gwilym Marlais – Dylan's middle name – was a preacher and a firebrand –*

Now we see the bashful boy DYLAN with his sister at a picnic.

MID DYLAN (V.O.): *Dylan grew up and played and picnicked with his sister Nancy and his friends. He was to write about Wales in the nineteen-thirties before the Second World War against Hitler.*

We return to SEQUENCES from 'WALES – GREEN MOUNTAIN, BLACK MOUNTAIN'. In his documentary, DYLAN wrote of his country. It showed the castles left by the old war (against England), as an introduction to the new war – steelworkers – dockers – pithead scenes from the Rhondda mines – sheep farming – Welsh chapels – children. It ended with the social and economic changes that industry brought to the valleys and the hardships of the Depression, which lasted until the arrival of new industry with the war.

COMMENTATOR (V.O.): *Morning is breaking over Wales at war. Not the long and faraway wild war of the mountain Welshmen and English kings, but the terrible near war of England and Wales and her brothers and sisters all over the earth, against the men who would murder man ...*

1

In the furnaces of Llanelly, in the roaring cauldrons of the Swansea Valley, in the stamp and clatter and glare of the black and red works where the fires never go out they fight with blinding, blasting rods and pistons, rams, they fight to the rhythm of iron forests thrusting between flames, they fight with the white hot muscles and arms of steel.

In the docks of the South they fight with ropes and crane and hoists, they load the ships to slide into the mined and death-sprung waters, and all the quays are alive, loud with war.

In the Rhondda Valley they fight with pick and shovel and drill, they fight the cruel obstinate dark rock middles of the mountains for minerals and metals. They go down into the splintered darkness of the mines, into the blind propped under-world with horses and canaries. They go down like ghosts in black, only their smiles are white.

Now we see SEQUENCES from another war documentary, 'WHEN WE BUILD AGAIN'. We see views of Birmingham in 1941 inside factories, over slum roofs to children playing games in the slum streets and housewives at their chores.

MID DYLAN (V.O.): *My father was a school-teacher and we lived in a Swansea villa. My family was not toiling in the shop-soiling factories –* (machine noises) *– We were not living in the slums and the foul air smutting the slip-shod roofs* (children's cries) *– And the games we played at school were not on the rascal paving stones of the ragamuffin streets.*

We return to DYLAN's script of 'WALES – GREEN MOUNTAIN, BLACK MOUNTAIN'.

COMMENTATOR (V.O.): *But the singing in the chapel is never grim or grey. The voices of quarrymen or shepherds, colliers or small farmers, tradesmen from the scorched valleys, or ploughmen from the long fields, the voices of children brought up to play Indians on the slagheaps, or pirates in the cattle-voiced meadows, are sweet and powerful, wild and gentle, as the weather over the mountains or the windlike movements of light and shadow through the high, chill streets ...*

We see the roadsign of CWMDONKIN DRIVE and then the exterior of the terrace house of the Thomas family, 5 Cwmdonkin Drive. BOY DYLAN looks out of the front bedroom. MOVE IN on him at the open window.

MID DYLAN (V.O.): *But Dylan knew none of this, when he was born in this bedroom in this house in 1914.*

Now we see the interior of the back bedroom of the house.

MID DYLAN (V.O.): *At the outbreak of the First World War ...*

And now in the front bedroom, BOY DYLAN is leaning on the windowsill, looking out on Cwmdonkin Park.

In a montage, we see views of the OLD Swansea in the nineteen-twenties, starting with Cwmdonkin Park.

MID DYLAN (V.O.): *Cwmdonkin Park, where he would play in the trees and bushes.*

We overlook the whole of old Swansea..

MID DYLAN (V.O.): *The old port lay below the hills behind the Town Hall.*

We MOVE along Craddock Street and DISSOLVE to the High Street and DISSOLVE to the trams trundling along their lines on two other streets, and follow with three more sights of trams moving along their paths.

MID DYLAN (V.O.): *And he could run down to the tramlines. The lines ran along the High Street. And the trams would trundle along Oxford Street and Union Street – rattling and shaking all the way – thunder in the drums of your ears.*

Now we see the Mumbles tramway taking the passengers to the railway station, where the train was ready to roll past the bay and arrive at the far Mumbles Pier.

The BOY DYLAN now pelts past a wooden sign saying FERN HILL and shakes the locked gates of the old Carmarthen farmhouse.

MID DYLAN (V.O.): *Ach, let me in.*

Now we look at the courtyard within.

MID DYLAN (V.O.): *Inside was the old courtyard, all pinkwash and doorgreen.*

Our eyes pass round the walled farmhouse in its coat of yellow wash sprawled round three sides of a court, with the farmyard and the outbuildings to one side. Like Cwmdonkin Drive, the farm stood on a slope and the ground dropped away sharply to a lower stream past an old flower-garden. And as the Swansea park, the farmhouse was surrounded by tall old trees, the survivors of that Milk Wood which once used to cover nearly all of ancient Wales. Although the house smelt of rotten wood and damp and animals, the kitchen was lamplit and warm, and Aunt ANNIE loved BOY DYLAN, and he played the summer days away in byre and field, on cart and hill.

MID DYLAN (V.O.): *Dylan loved his Aunt Annie at the farm at Fern Hill, and she loved him, and he would write a poem about his happiness there.*

OLD DYLAN (V.O.): *Now as I was young and easy under the apple boughs*
About the lilting house and happy as the grass was green,
The night above the dingle starry,
Time let me hail and climb

3

Golden in the heydays of his eyes,
And honoured among wagons I was prince of the apple towns
And once below a time I lordly had the trees and leaves
Trail with daisies and barley
Down the rivers of the windfall light.

And as I was green and carefree, famous among the barns
About the happy yard and singing as the farm was home,
In the sun that is young once only,
Time let me play and be
Golden in the mercy of his means,
And green and golden I was huntsman and herdsman, the calves
Sang to my horn, the foxes on the hills barked clear and cold,
And the sabbath rang slowly
In the pebbles of the holy streams.

All the sun long it was running, it was lovely, the hay
Fields high as the house, the tunes from the chimneys, it was air
And playing, lovely and watery

And fire green as grass.
And nightly under the simple stars
As I rode to sleep the owls were bearing the farm away,
All the moon long I heard, blessed among stables, the night-jars

Flying with the ricks, and the horses
Flashing into the dark ...

Over the poem, we see more SHOTS of the farms of Wales under the mountains, particularly –

– Sheep pouring over a bank and through a gap in a hedge round a pasture.

– A farmer's wife knitting an enormous scarf, full of holes. Her cat walks over the endless wool comforter.

– Under a hill, a herd of cows moves and moos on their way to milking.

– High on the hill, a white mare and her foal graze in the moonlight.

– A huge Cow-woman talks to the cows, coming into the yard.

– She is kissed by a Farmhand.

– From her stool, she milks the udder of a cow into a pail.

– Also many SHOTS of BOY DYLAN running, laughing, bursting out from leaves and straw –

Now BOY DYLAN runs towards the door of Paraclete chapel in Swansea.

MID DYLAN (V.O.): *The boy also learned the Bible and the hwyl from the fire-and-brimstone preaching of his uncle, the Reverend Rees –*

Inside the Paraclete schoolroom, we show a clock and a banner stating THE GIFT OF GOD IS ETERNAL LIFE.

MID DYLAN (V.O.): *Though he didn't like Sunday School Lessons under time and the promise he'd live for ever.*

The BOY DYLAN in shorts and jacket with a satchel runs towards the front door of his terrace house and bangs on the door.

MID DYLAN (V.O.): *But back in the streets of Swansea, the boy Dylan ran home, not thinking about the Depression and the dole queue. And who was waiting for him inside?*

Three portraits of the mother and sister and the schoolmaster father of DYLAN THOMAS are flashed on screen.

MID DYLAN (V.O.): *His family, naturally.*

MRS FLORENCE THOMAS is packing a full suitcase.

MID DYLAN (V.O.): *He described his mother Florence in his autobiographical work ADVENTURES IN THE SKIN TRADE – "stout, safe, confident, buried in her errands."*

NANCY THOMAS is dancing with a man's suit of clothes.

MID DYLAN (V.O.): *His sister, with all the long legs and the Young Liberals' dances, and the boys you brought home for supper on Sunday evenings and Lionel you kissed on the porch.*

MR D.J. THOMAS is correcting examinations.

MID DYLAN (V.O.): *"Most of the history sheets on the table were already marked and damned in his schoolmaster father's violent writing."*

A dog sleeps in a basket.

MID DYLAN (V.O.): *"And Tinker, the aunt-faced pom."*

Now we watch the schoolmaster still working at his papers.

MID DYLAN (V.O.): *Oh yes, I remember him well, the boy you are*
        searching for:
        he looked like most boys, no better, brighter, or more
        respectful;
        he cribbed, mitched, spilt ink, rattled his desk and
        garbled his lessons with the worst of them;
        he could smudge, hedge, smirk, wriggle, wince,
        whimper, blarney, badger, blush, deceive, be
        devious, stammer, improvise, assume

offended dignity or righteous indignation as though
to the manner born ...

We see the exterior of the old Swansea Grammar school and children running there and fighting in the playground.

MID DYLAN (V.O.):   *... he scuffled at prayers,*
he interpolated, smugly the time-honoured wrong
irreverent words into the morning hymns,
he helped to damage the headmaster's rhubarb,
was thirty-third in trigonometry,
and, as might be expected, edited the School
Magazine.

Now a caricature of YOUNG DYLAN appears before we glimpse over his shoulder his hand opening on a desktop the cover of the Swansea School Magazine – EDITOR D.M. THOMAS.

Now we see Warmley House, where DYLAN's close friend lived.

MID DYLAN (V.O.): *His early and best friend was Daniel Jones, who took him home to Warmley, which chimed with music and the arts.*

And the cover of NEW ERA magazine –

MID DYLAN (V.O.): *There they edited their first magazine.*

And DYLAN played the part of Oliver Cromwell.

MID DYLAN (V.O.): *And acted in plays ...*

VERNON WATKINS was another companion on land and in water.

MID DYLAN (V.O.): *And Dylan's other great friend was Vernon Watkins ... They swam together ...*

The two friends go at each other verbally.

MID DYLAN (V.O.): *And they would argue all the time all their lives.*

Back in Cwmdonkin Park is the magical territory of a small child. The white-bearded PARK-KEEPER in uniform fails to guard the place. BOY DYLAN bursts through the clumps of trees and dashes past the iron fountain.

MID DYLAN (V.O.): *And Cwmdonkin Park outside Dylan's front door was "full of terrors and treasures ... as many secret places, caverns and forests, prairies and deserts, as a county somewhere at the end of the sea."*

Now a HUNCHBACK drags his way through the Park. He looks up at a tall tree and imagines it as MARLENE DIETRICH, before it passes back to leaves again. He wanders away.

MID DYLAN (V.O.): *He made all day until bell time*
A woman figure without fault
Straight as a young elm
Straight and tall from his crooked bones

That she might stand in the night
After the locks and chains
All night in the unmade park
After the railings and the shrubberies
The birds the grass the trees the lake
And the wildboys innocent as strawberries
Had followed the hunchback
To his kennel in the dark.

The young DYLAN THOMAS is smiling, then playing croquet. He merges into MID DYLAN, going back to the Queen's Free House Hotel in Swansea in search of his youth.

MID DYLAN (V.O.): *In his sad radio play, 'Return Journey', Dylan Thomas saw himself at the end of his life and his tether, going back to Swansea to look for the young man he was then. "The bar was just opening ... I said Good morning ..."*

A BARMAID is polishing the counter vigorously as though it were a rare and valuable piece of Swansea china. A CUSTOMER is sitting on a stool. There is the background noise of other customers chatting, as MID DYLAN comes in.

MID DYLAN (V.O.): *A pint of bitter please ... I wonder whether you remember a friend of mine? He always used to come to this bar, some years ago. Every morning, about this time.*

BARMAID: *What's his name?*

MID DYLAN (V.O.): *Young Thomas –*

FLASH – We see DAVID HEMMINGS in a felt hat as the young DYLAN THOMAS.

BARMAID: *Lots of Thomases come here it's a kind of home from home for Thomases what's he look like?*

MID DYLAN (V.O.): *He'd be about seventeen or eighteen ...*

BARMAID: *I was seventeen once ...*

MID DYLAN (V.O.): *... and above medium height. Above medium height for Wales, I mean, he's five foot six and a half. Speaks rather fancy; truculent; plausible; a bit of a shower-off; plus-fours and no breakfast, you know ... a bombastic adolescent provincial Bohemian with a thick-knotted artist's tie made out of his sister's scarf, she never knew where it had gone, and a cricket-shirt dyed bottle-green; a gabbing, ambitious, mock-tough, pretentious young man; and mole-y, too.*

BARMAID: *There's words what d'you want to find him for I wouldn't touch him with a barge-pole ... would you?*

FLASHES – DAVID HEMMINGS as the young DYLAN THOMAS is leaving home and the Swansea docks.

The CUSTOMER on the bar stool intervenes in the pub.

CUSTOMER: *I seem to remember a chap like you described. There couldn't be two like him let's hope. He used to work as a reporter. Down the Three Lamps I used to see him. Lifting his ikkle elbow.*

MID DYLAN (V.O.): *What's the Three Lamps like now?*

CUSTOMER: *It isn't like anything. It isn't there. It's nothing mun. You remember Ben Evans's stores? It's right next door to that. Ben Evans isn't there either.*

There are scenes of ruined houses and shops, from the time when the Germans blitzed Swansea in the Second World War.

MID DYLAN (V.O.): *I walked down High Street, where all the shops had been. Eddershaw Furnishers, Curry's Bicycles, Donegal Clothing Company, Doctor Scholl's, Burton Tailors, W.H. Smith, Boots Cash Chemists, Leslie's Stores, Upson's Shoes, Prince of Wales, Tucker's Fish, Stead & Simpson – all the shops bombed and vanished. Past the hole in space where Hodges & Clothiers had been, down Castle Street, past the remembered, invisible shops, and in the falling winter morning I walked on through the havoc'd centre where once a very young man I knew had mucked about as chirpy as a sparrow after the sips and titbits and small change of the town.*

In a SERIES OF SHOTS, MID DYLAN is seen as he walks past the Castle and the Museum and the Antelope Tavern to the Swansea docks.

MID DYLAN (V.O.): *The Castle was already ruined, you see, but the Museum was still standing – should be in a museum – and the Antelope down by the docks, where I played darts, if I could stick the cork, like a bomb on target – And then down onto the wharves, where they were still working, loading the ships and the barges, all sooty from the evenfall of the dark. I stopped a man whose face I thought I recognized from a long time ago. I said: I wonder if you can tell me ...*

Backed by two cranes and framed by two coal slagheaps, a man is stopped by MID DYLAN with his back to us. The PASSER-BY wears an overcoat.

PASSER-BY: *Yes.*

MID DYLAN (V.O.): *I said: If you can tell me whether you used to know a chap called Young Thomas. He worked on the Post and used to wear an overcoat sometimes with the check lining inside out so that you could play giant draughts on him . He wore a conscious woodbine, too ...*

PASSER-BY: *What d'you mean, conscious woodbine?*

MID DYLAN (V.O.): *... And a perched pork pie with a peacock feather and he tried to slouch like a newshawk?*

PASSER BY: *Oh, him! He owes me half a crown. I haven't seen him since the old Kardomah days. He wasn't a reporter then, he'd just left the grammar school. Him drinking coffee-dashes and arguing the toss.*

MID DYLAN (V.O.): *What about?*

PASSER-BY: *Music and poetry and painting and politics. Einstein and Epstein, Stravinsky and Greta Garbo, death and religion, Picasso and girls ...*

MID DYLAN (V.O.): *And then?*

PASSER-BY: *Communism, symbolism, Bradman, Braque, the Watch Committee, free love, free beer, murder, Michelangelo, ping-pong, ambition, Sibelius, and girls ...*

MID DYLAN (V.O.): *Is that all?*

Over another FLASH of HEMMINGS as YOUNG DYLAN we hear:

PASSER-BY: *How Dan Jones was going to compose the most prodigious symphony, Fred Janes paint the most miraculously meticulous picture of Vernon Watkins, and Young Thomas write the most boiling poems, how they would ring the bells of London and paint it like a tart ...*

Now we see the portrait of VERNON WATKINS by ALFRED JANES.

MID DYLAN (V.O.): *And after that?*

INSERT in the conversation of the PASSER-BY a sequence of early film erotic stills, mainly of MARLENE DIETRICH.

PASSER-BY: *Oh the hissing of the butt-ends in the drains of the coffee dashes and the tinkle and the gibble-gabble of the morning young lounge lizards as they talked about Augustus John, Emil Jannings, Carnera, Dracula, Amy Johnson, trial marriage, pocket-money, the Welsh sea, the London stars, King Kong, anarchy, darts, T.S. Eliot, and girls ... Duw, it's cold!*

MID DYLAN (V.O.): *But what else did young Thomas do before he rang the bells of London and painted it like a tart?*

Calling himself Sam Bennett, DYLAN THOMAS wrote of smashing up the parlour of his genteel family at 5 Cwmdonkin Drive in ADVENTURES IN THE SKIN TRADE.

DYLAN's Mother and Sister pack his going-to-London suitcase, and all go to bed.

MID DYLAN (V.O.): *Dylan had a fantasy of how he left his home in Swansea. In his unfinished novel ADVENTURES IN THE SKIN TRADE, after the family went to bed and time passed, he called himself Samuel*

Bennett and smashed up the parlour. He never wanted to be able to go home again.

We see the clock tick by and YOUNG DYLAN destroy the family home and leave on the dawn train to London to learn the seven deadly sins. On the journey, he says:

MID DYLAN (V.O.): *Even in the first moment of his guilt and shame, he remembered to put out his tongue and taste the track of the tears. Still crying, he said, "It's salt. It's very salt. Just like in my poems."*

Arriving in London, YOUNG DYLAN is picked up by a group of Soho spongers, who take him on a drunken dance in the rain.

MID DYLAN (V.O.): *Look at London flying by me, buses and glow-worms, umbrellas and lamp posts, cigarettes and eyes under the water doorways, I am dancing with three strangers down Edgware Road in the rain, cried Samuel to the gliding boy around him. Light and without will as a suit of feathers, he held on to their arms, and the umbrella rode above them like a bird ... My place is among the beggars and the outlaws. With power and violence Samuel Bennett destroys the whole artifice of society in his latest novel, In the Bowels.*

"Piccadilly Circus. Centre of the world. See the man picking his nose under the lamp post? That's the Prime Minister."

In an interview, MERVYN LEVY talks about DYLAN's first days in London,

MID DYLAN (V.O.): *The artist Mervyn Levy also came from Swansea and was Dylan's flatmate in those prewar days in Chelsea.*

MERVYN LEVY: *He was a very bad stable companion due to he didn't like paying his rent.*

We see a portrait of DYLAN THOMAS by ALFRED JANES, then the large JANES holds the YOUNG DYLAN upside down to shake the rent money out of his pockets.

MERVYN LEVY: *This – uh – irritated him greatly, not unnaturally, but like most of us in those days he didn't really have any money but somebody had to find the rent. The chap who always looked after the rent and who was the most capable and the most businesslike was Arthur Janes, of course, who has drawn and painted Dylan a number of times, and very often it meant that Fred Janes was a great big strong burly bloke who would simply collar Dylan when he was behind with the rent and literally, I remember on one occasion, turn him upside down and shake out whatever money there was in Dylan on to the floor of one of the rooms in Colherne Road – Dylan screaming and raving and fighting and ranting and said "Let go, you great big bully, you rotten bloody coward," and what not.*

The youthful DYLAN THOMAS and the young writer PAMELA HANSFORD JOHNSON are seen bathing by the Welsh seaside.

MID DYLAN (V.O.): *Then Dylan became engaged to the very respectable young writer, Miss Pamela Hansford Johnson, who remembered him:*

In an interview the late PAMELA HANSFORD JOHNSON describes DYLAN THOMAS and the London of the time and their relationship.

PAMELA HANSFORD JOHNSON: *He was very excited about the publication of 18 Poems – he took tremendous care to choose them. He was quite determined that he wasn't having any nonsensical title. He was very keen on that so he said mine's going to be called 18 Poems. I'm not going to have a preface. I'm not going to have any photograph but when it came you have to realise there was rather a long time lag between it being accepted and the book coming out of course. During that time he had become fairly well known. I used to sit with him – we used to have happy evenings in the gardens of the Six Bells, the pub in Chelsea which then opened onto a bowling green and had a little fountain and we would talk and then he would suddenly say I got a wonderful phrase and write it down and then he would sometimes say let's have a game, let's write a poem together, you see. He did drink very much for effect at that time. It was very strange. I remember that he would fake it and I'd been sitting with him in the Six Bells and we had something very modest like a pint a piece during the whole evening, very modest, then gone out into the street – met some of his friends and Dylan would immediately have played drunk – it was somehow the romantic thing to be.*

Over a SERIES of pictures of London landmarks, ending on a policeman halting traffic, we hear:

MID DYLAN (V.O.): *Dylan took to Chelsea and London like a drake to drink and ducks. He lived by cadging, reviewing and publishing a few poems. He was continually short of sleeping places near to his pubs, and he would find himself in a convenient bed more often than a chosen one. Once he said: "Oh God, I'm so tired of sleeping with women I don't even like." Asked why he drank so much, he said: "Because they expect it of me" – until he came to a stop.*

Now we have a MONTAGE of Surrealist film STILLS, including MAX ERNST's 1936 Poster for a London Exhibition.

MID DYLAN (V.O.): *Dylan's early prose and poetry were becoming obscure and clotted, because he fell under the influence of the Dadaists and the Surrealists, particularly the films of Luís Buñuel. At their 1936 Exhibition in London, he was outclassed by Salvador Dali and Max Ernst and others.*

He only passed round boiled string in a teacup. He ended up as unlikely and uncomfortable as Cocteau's Blood of a Poet.

YOUNG CAITLIN (ANGHARAD REES) meets with MID DYLAN in a pork-pie hat in front of a walled street. They are dancing and joyous and full of love.

MID DYLAN (V.O.): *Back on the town in Soho, Dylan was to meet the love of his life, soon to be his wife. She was Caitlin Macnamara, a free-style dancer with a wild spirit in her.*

During the next VOICE OVER, we see four portraits
  – A photograph of the aged painter AUGUSTUS JOHN.
  – A self-portrait by Augustus John.
  – A portrait of CAITLIN by Augustus John.
  – A colour portrait of DYLAN THOMAS.
  – FOUR STILLS of the young lovers, CAITLIN and DYLAN.

MID DYLAN (V.O.): *She was the mistress of the aged painter, Augustus John, who still thought he was young – and so he painted himself as well as painting Caitlin. After a drunken fight in Wales, John knocked down Dylan. But the poet ran away with Caitlin and married her and wrote to her: "We'll always be young and unwise together. There is, I suppose, in the eyes of the They, a sort of sweet madness about you and me, a sort of mad bewilderment and astonishment oblivious to the Nasties and the Meanies." But Mussolini and Hitler were pushing Europe into a Second World War –*

A long SERIES of QUICK SHOTS shows the opening of the Second World War with the Italian fighting machines and the first bombing raids. These black-and-white SHOTS DISSOLVE into a red Poster of thumbs down to burning London.

MID DYLAN (V.O.): *And such wonder and spoilt innocence couldn't last into the realities of marriage, and later, three children. The remarkable thing was that Dylan and Caitlin didn't change their life-styles much, at least not the pubbing and the boozing and even the casual sex, when they had the opportunity and a quid or two. Why not live for the day and leave the bills for tomorrow?*

We see a caricature of HITLER as a stage juggler, then of factory workers taking their tea under a bomb, then of the beginning of the Blitz.

MID DYLAN (V.O.): *At first, the outbreak of hostilities in Europe seemed quite a laugh. There was a phoney war in France – and no bombs. Then they began to fall – even on Soho –*

Now we see scenes of an imperial procession with the Life Guards riding by, a Guards Officer carried off on a stretcher and the Royal Coach ambling along.

MID DYLAN (V.O.): *Dylan didn't want to fight. He hated ceremony and dressing up. Luckily, he wasn't called up to be a soldier because of asthma and poor health.*

A LOW CARTOON shows HITLER and MUSSOLINI not knowing whether to attack Moscow or the Western Allies.

MID DYLAN (V.O.): *Anyway, he thought the whole conflict was stupid. Where was anyone going?*

From war FOOTAGE, we see Soho signs and shops, ending on three TAKES of the pub in Dean Street, the YORK MINSTER.

MID DYLAN (V.O.): *Soho was the air-raid shelter – And the best of the shelters – was the York Minster, the French pub.*

Inside the pub in a booth, in front of the aged photographs of stars and boxers and the absinthe signs, MID DYLAN is drinking and arguing with CAITLIN. Occasionally, bombs crump in the background, by the church of St. Anne's Soho, which was destroyed.

MID DYLAN: *Here's how, Cat.*

CAITLIN: *How what?*

MID DYLAN: *How to survive the Blitz. Bombs don't hit pubs. Or we wouldn't be here.*

CAITLIN: *We're here because they still have beer, have beer, have beer. And because you aren't in the army. Asthma, my eye. More like smoker's coughin'. They one they'll carry you off in.*

MID DYLAN: (coughing) *You'll see. You'll be sorry. I'm worse than Keats. I'm a T.B. poet.*

CAITLIN: *A D.T.s poet. Where did we get our name from? The Dylan Thomases. The D.T.s.*

MID DYLAN: *I'm doing my war work.*

CAITLIN: *You're fighting by making documentaries, is it? About a hole in the ground. No, it's not a mousehole. It's a bomb.*

MID DYLAN: *I'm good for morale. And good for the morgue. You'll see, Cat. You'll see too late.*

CAITLIN: *And what about your bloody poetry? Isn't that why we have to live on debts and biscuits?*

MID DYLAN turns to CAMERA to lament his lack of writing his poems.

MID DYLAN: *Oh no work of words now for three lean months in the*
                                                          bloody

Belly of the rich year and the big purse of my body
I bitterly take to task my poverty and craft:

To take to give is all, return what is hungrily given
Puffing the pounds of manna up through the dew to heaven
The lovely gift of the gab bangs back on a blind shaft.

MID DYLAN goes into a horrible spasm of coughing, which ends with him spitting on the floor. He examines the result with gloomy satisfaction.

MID DYLAN: *It's blood, that's the stuff.*

CAITLIN: *It's bloody self-pity, that is.*

MID DYLAN: *I'll get rich from the films, just you see. Cinema is my forte, not bloody poetry.*

CAITLIN: *If the war don't get us first. And it will.*

We see a short SEQUENCE of war Posters and more scenes of London burning as explosions sound.

MID DYLAN (V.O.): *They went on loving and bickering and talking too much – They had no money to spend, even on rations – and of course a bomb never did fall upon them in the end.*

Over the CREDIT TITLES of the documentary 'BALLOON SITE 568', we see a squad of WAAFS marching out of a hangar. Then two SHOTS of Barrage Balloons, followed by other SHOTS of women in the Air Force.

MID DYLAN (V.O.): *While Caitlin and her babies camped in Chelsea and Hammersmith and later in Oxford and New Quay in Wales, Dylan travelled, writing war documentaries for Strand Films, including one about barrage balloon operators from the Women's Auxiliary Air Force. On a reviewing stand with the Lady Commandant, Dylan said: "You have the most superb body, ma'am (long pause) of women." Writing documentaries refined Dylan's prose. He had to write for a mass audience. And it made his poetry less obscure. In fact, though he wrote few poems during the war, some were very good. He also wrote on the Blitz on Coventry.*

In another documentary, 'A CITY REBORN', DYLAN describes how the factories and houses and cathedral of Coventry were reduced to rubble and ashes, and how the place would rise again.

MID DYLAN (V.O.): *On the 14th November 1940, it became a City of Destruction. For three nights the German bombers attacked in their fullest force. This introduced a new word into the vocabulary of mass-murder; to – Coventrate.*

Large areas of the City were devastated.

The hospital was destroyed.
Forty churches.
Fourteen schools.
60,000 houses were damaged out of a total of 75,000.
1,252 men, women and children lost their lives.
The monastery that grew into a little town. The little town that grew into a famous place of guilds and crafts and medieval ceremony, into a rich trade town, into a great centre of industry, into a burned, bombed city – it didn't die.

We see firemen trying to douse the burning Docklands. We hear 'A Refusal to Mourn the Death by Fire, of a Child in London'.

OLD DYLAN (V.O.): *The majesty and burning of the child's death.*
I shall not murder
The mankind of her going with a grave truth
Nor blaspheme down the stations of the breath
With any further
Elegy of innocence and youth.

Deep with the first dead lies London's daughter,
Robed in the long friends,
The grains beyond age, the dark veins of her mother,
Secret by the unmourning water
Of the riding Thames.
After the first death, there is no other.

Now we are introduced to early battle SEQUENCES from the documentary 'THESE ARE THE MEN'.

MID DYLAN (V.O.): *Dylan's most successful and witty propaganda film was 'THESE ARE THE MEN'.*

COMMENTATOR (V.O.): *We are the makers the workers the wounded*
the dying the dead
The blind the frostbitten the burned the legless
the mad
Sons of the earth who are fighting and hating
and killing now
In snow and sand and heat and mud,
In the streets of never-lost Stalingrad
In the spine-freezing cold of the Caucasus

In the jungles of Papua
In the tank-churned black slime of Tunisia.
We are the makers the workers the starving
the slaves
In Greece and China and Poland, digging our
own graves.
Who sent us to kill, to be killed, to lose what
we love?
Widowed our women, unfathered our sons,
broke the hearts of our homes?
Who dragged us out, out of our beds and
houses and workshops
Into a battle-yard of spilt blood and spilt bones?
Who set us at the throats of our comrades?
Who is to blame?
What set man against man?
Shout, shout, shout out their name!

Against SEQUENCES from Leni Reifenstahl's 'Triumph of the Will', her praise of the Nazis at their Nuremberg Rally, DYLAN set confessions by the leaders of the Third Reich in a brilliant parody. Three figures mount the platform at Nuremberg. Amid waving flags, we see HITLER, HESS and GOERING. They join other Nazi leaders.

COMMENTATOR (V.O.): *These are the men – these are to blame.*

HITLER raves in German. Over his voice we hear a false English translation:

HITLER: *I was born of poor parents.*
I grew into a discontented and neurotic child.
My lungs were bad, my mother spoilt me and secured my
exemption from military service.
Consider my triumphant path to power.
(the crowd roars approval)
I took up art.
I gave up art because I was incompetent.
I became a bricklayer's labourer.
A housepainter.
A paperhanger.
A peddler of pictures.
A lance-corporal,
A spy on socialists and communists,
A hater of Jews and Trade Unions,
A political prisoner,

But my work was known.
Patriotic industrial magnates financed me.
CROWD: *Heil! Heil!*
HITLER: *I am a normal man,*
I do not like meat, drink or women.
CROWD: *Heil! Heil!*
HITLER: *Neurosis, charlatanism, bombast, anti-socialism,*
Hate of the Jews, treachery, murder, race-insanity.
I am the leader of the German people.
CROWD: *Heil! Heil!*

Now we see the massed Gestapo, marching, led by HIMMLER.

COMMENTATOR (V.O.): *And these are the men, the young men,*
the callow boys
Who have been taught the knuckle-duster and
the rubber hose.
You are only young once: you could have
learned to love;
You have learned to maim the weak and to
spit on the Jews.
You have been taught to betray your country
and your people,
Your own flesh and blood, your comrades
all over the earth;
Young men like you have hacked and blasted
The lands and the homes of strangers who did
you no harm,
Burned men and women alive
And left a slug-trail behind you of terror and
death.
You obeyed your leader's word.
You must suffer his reward.

From the marching Gestapo, MOVE to German prisoners being marched away in Africa and Russia.

COMMENTATOR (V.O.): *And the betrayers are betrayed, and the*
promises of victory
Turn stale and sour under African sun and
Russian snow.

German soldier corpses lie dead in the Russian winter.

COMMENTATOR (V.O.): *Where is your triumph now in the purgatories*
of Stalingrad?
How many of you will never return to the
towns and villages you know?

FADE on masses of wooden crosses over the graves of German
soldiers.

Now we are shown masses of workers pouring into factories and
offices and stations on their daily progress.

MID DYLAN (V.O.): *Dylan himself spoke on how everybody wanted to go*
home, once the war was over. The documentary was called 'WHEN WE
BUILD AGAIN'.

DYLAN THOMAS (V.O.): *Here are people in Britain – the people – people*
pouring in the evening from the roaring factory, people in the big cities
bustling from offices with umbrellas and bags and satchels in a homewards
hubbub to the suburb, coal death flocking back from the midnight colours
underground at the pits, gleaming out into the restless teeming streets from
the quays and the wharves and the engine-shops of the great-thronged dark,
the funnelled people's town of ships, from crowds on the island and queues at
the stops, shopping, bus-hopping, scurrying, hurrying out of the terrible
traffic clamour into the dimmer, never-still echoing station, where out of all
of us, all the people, look at three soldiers going home.

In a SEQUENCE at the Welsh seaside town of New Quay, we end on a
bungalow named MAJODA, and then see CAITLIN and her children
relaxing on the beach.

MID DYLAN (V.O.): *Dylan managed to get his family back to Wales at the*
end of the war to a bungalow called Majoda in New Quay. There were three
children – Llewellyn – and Aeron called Aeronwy – and baby Colm. If Dylan
thought the war was over in seaside Wales, he was wrong.

From 'WHEN WE BUILD AGAIN', we START ON a SOLDIER
hitching a van lift from under a Guinness sign and going to the suburbs.

MID DYLAN (V.O.): *Soldiers were also returning.*

DYLAN THOMAS (V.O.): *Going our way mister? Up the streets like dingy*
corridors through the straggled drab districts that crawl from the great
centres, out of the city rattling over tramlines, out of the dank grey
thoroughfares, into the wider spaces, where trees are still green, and the only
smoke comes from houses ...

The SOLDIER leaves the city for the countryside. He is going home.

MID DYLAN (V.O.): *A soldier came back to New Quay, and he was jealous*
about his wife and Dylan. After a fight outside The Black Lion –

We view The BLACK LION pub, outside and inside, with AERONWY THOMAS playing CAITLIN and MID DYLAN playing her poet husband.

MID DYLAN (V.O.): *The soldier burst into Majoda with a sub-machine gun and a grenade, and he peppered the walls and ceilings with shots. He was disarmed by Dylan, who managed to protect his family at last. Indeed, at this time, Dylan was writing his best poetry. The year of the end of the war and his return to Wales brought about the flowering of his genius. From the slow killing of the city, he had to take refuge in his own country to think and be the bard he wanted to be.*

Now we see together the actors, who serve as MID DYLAN and CAITLIN/AERONWY, as they play by a rowboat by the Welsh sea with their three children, a boy and a girl and a baby. And we hear CAITLIN saying DYLAN'S poem for his firstborn LLEWELYN, 'This Side of the Truth':

CAITLIN/AERONWY (V.O.):   *This side of the truth,*
       You may not see, my son,
       King of your blue eyes
       In the blinding country of youth,
       That all is undone,
       Under the unminding skies,
       Of innocence and guilt
       Before you move to make
       One gesture of the heart or head,
       Is gathered and spilt
       Into the winding dark
       Like the dust of the dead.

In an interview at the Boathouse at Laugharne, where she lived with her family as a child, AERONWY THOMAS talks with moving memories of her loving and exuberant father.

Now MID DYLAN goes into the old headquarters of the British Broadcasting Company at Langham Place in London.

MID DYLAN (V.O.): *But the family peace in Wales was continually ruined by the need of Dylan to earn money in London to keep himself from ruin. He found it not in writing films now, but in writing and performing for the B.B.C. He had been a young actor in Swansea, and his voice, which was growing more rich and plummy as he became plumper, was a success over the air-waves.*

Now MID DYLAN enters the wireless pub, The GEORGE. His cheeks are pouchier, his speech and tone slower.

MID DYLAN (V.O.): *After the performances at the B.B.C., Dylan would gather in 'The George' with the other actors and producers, to drink till closing time.*

MID DYLAN is sitting in a wooden pub booth, draining his beer-mug.

MID DYLAN (V.O.): *One night, with Louis MacNeice and Richard Burton, the question was, What was the greatest poem in the world? MacNeice spoke his own 'Bar-room Matins' while Burton did a bit of Hamlet. But Dylan said:*

MID DYLAN: *I will tell you what is the greatest poem in the world. Not one of mine, but ... (swelling his chest) ...*

> *I am*
> *Thou art*
> *He, she and it is*
> *We are*
> *You are*
> *They are*
> *That is the greatest poem in the world.*

MID DYLAN (V.O.): *He won a free pint.*

We MOVE DOWN from the tower of Magdalen College at Oxford to show boats and punts on the river.

MID DYLAN (V.O.): *In his bardic way, Dylan was still looking for patrons to keep him and his family. He found one in the wealthy Margaret Taylor, the wife of an Oxford historian, who taught at Magdalen College here.*

Holywell Ford is shown and the TAYLOR house behind a garden. Deer graze by Magdalen College.

MID DYLAN (V.O.): *She lent them a dank summerhouse on the River Cherwell at the bottom of her garden in Holywell Ford. Watching from his writing caravan, Dylan could look over another iron fence to the animals caged in the deer park of his Oxford College hosts.*

DYLAN now passes the Bodleian Library at Oxford.

MID DYLAN (V.O.): *His way was not to visit the Bodleian Library with its priceless manuscripts. He preferred the pubs of London, to escape from the crying children and Caitlin, who could not stand being kept by a rival woman –*

After showing a PATRICK PROCTOR painting of ANDREW SINCLAIR drinking in the Soho Colony Room, bar scenes of the 'forties and Soho drinkers we end on ANDREW slouched and drunk in the Salubrious Pub in Swansea.

ANDREW: *He was lampooned by a fellow Fitzrovian in a poem:*

> *I saw him sitting in the Gargoyle,*
> *Very drunk and very ill:*
> *Fields of Fern Hill green and golden*
> *Deep the shadows of Bunhill.*
> *Double whisky! Double brandy!*
> *Double dyed is hard to kill.*
> *Where is Vernon? Where is Louis?*
> *Have I slept with you before?*
> *Sticks or paper, match or shovel*
> *Cannot make an old flame roar*

The MERMAID pub was a regular DYLAN drinking haunt.

MID DYLAN (V.O.): *And on his way back to Laugharne by train, he'd drink in the Mermaid in Mumbles.*

We look from the sea towards the Boathouse at Laugharne.

MID DYLAN (V.O.): *Dylan and Caitlin and the three children were living in a Boathouse on the estuary –*

Five more scenes inside and outside the Boathouse are shown.

MID DYLAN (V.O.): *Dylan wrote to Margaret Taylor, thanking her for the peace she had bought for him. "O to sit there, lost, found, alone in the universe, at home, at last, the people all with their arms open! ... you climb the stones to see river, sea, cormorants nesting like thin headstones, the cockle-women webfoot, and the undead, round Pendine head, streaming like trippers up into seaside sky, making a noise like St. Giles Fair, silent as all the electric chairs and bells of my nerves as I think, here, of the best town, the best house, the only castle, the mapped, measured, unhabited, drained, garaged, townhalled, pubbed and churched, shopped, gulled and estuaried one state of happiness!"*

Now we see inside the Boathouse shed, where DYLAN wrote.

MID DYLAN (V.O.): *Dylan did his writing in a shed on stilts at the back of the boathouse. He pinned family photographs on the wooden wall as he wrote his poems – They all ate under a Welsh dresser, hoping the china wouldn't fall or be chucked at each other.*

Over a MONTAGE of photographs of DYLAN writing and working at his table on a poem page – his wastepaper basket and ashtray full – we hear:

OLD DYLAN (V.O.):

> *In my craft or sullen art*
> *Exercised in the still night*
> *When only the moon rages*
> *And the lovers lie abed*
> *With all their griefs in their arms,*
> *I labour by singing light*

Not for ambition or bread
Or the strut and trade of charms
On the ivory stages
But for the common wages
Of their most secret heart.

Not for the proud man apart
From the raging moon I write
On these spindrift pages
Nor for the towering dead
With their nightingales and psalms
But for the lovers, their arms
Round the griefs of the ages,
Who pay no praise or wages
Nor heed my craft or art.

The Main Street at Laugharne leads to a Pump in Grist Square, then to white-fronted houses and Brown's Hotel.

MID DYLAN (V.O.): *And then Dylan and Caitlin went slowly along the main street to the village pump, where the gossips were, and beer at Brown's Hotel.*

Inside Brown's, the ageing MID DYLAN is sitting in a pub booth with CAITLIN (ANGHARAD REES), arguing bitterly, across empty and full beer mugs.

MID DYLAN: *Did you hear the one about the man in the pub, went to take a leak, left a note on his beer, I'VE SPAT IN IT, and he came back to find scribbled on the bottom, SO HAVE I.*

CAITLIN: *That was me. I'm not letting you go to America. You won't come back. You're past it, see.*

MID DYLAN: *And the Irish firing squad? They don't form a line, they form a circle. About turn. Point their guns inwards. And fire! Only the victim survives.*

CAITLIN: *They'll eat you alive in New York.*

MID DYLAN: *Oh yes, they'll gobble me up for breakfast. I'm so bloody famous, am I?*

CAITLIN: *Everybody wants a piece of you now. But you can't even pay the bloody bills. I'll have to go on the streets, I will.*

MID DYLAN: *There's only one street in Laugharne. And no takers.*

CAITLIN: *Don't you be so bloody cocksure. You won't go over there.*

MID DYLAN: *I have to pay the bills. And fuel the engine. Here's to you, blithe spirit!*

(drains his beer)

Did you hear that one about Lorca, before they shot him in Spain? He had poet's block, you see, just like me. So in front of the firing squad, they make him dig his grave. But when they come to shoot him, the officer finds him smiling. And why? "Well," he says, "a plot at last."

(pause)

I'm going to lecture in America, you know. He who is about to die, salute me.

(pause)

I'm never going to grow old, am I?

At a podium in a lecture hall at an American university, OLD DYLAN is speaking, booming and pouchy and aged.

OLD DYLAN: *I welcome you, culture vultures, to this pot-boiling lyrical extravaganza, word-binge or bender. Standing here as I do in my Sunday best in one of the Dean Butler's university shirts, the self-styled Rimbaud of Cwmdonkin Drive, Swansea, or poor man's Charles Laughton, above average height and fierce – above average height for Wales, I mean, five foot six and a half, with the face of an excommunicated cherub, a nose that's polished every day, a body when clothed once so cruelly described as looking like an unmade bed, a staggering swagger but spoiling for a fight with any pavement bold enough to take me on, and a fancy pulpit-posh voice with brass knobs on, speaking three languages, English, B.B.C. Third Programme and Saloon. In my poems, that I recite to anyone, such as yourselves, a bunch of eccentrics voluntarily cornered, I've had my say, all I'm doing is saying it again, giving the works the works. In this first poem, which is a birthday poem, I went to bed at twenty-nine, I awoke at thirty, and took the New Quay countryside by surprise, with an early morning walk when it wasn't looking:-*

At dawn, we see the Welsh countryside and sea views around New Quay and Pembrokeshire, which are INTERCUT with OLD DYLAN speaking his 'Poem in October':–

OLD DYLAN (V.O.): *It was my thirtieth year to heaven*

Woke to my hearing from harbour and neighbour wood
And the mussel pooled and the heron
Priested shore
The morning beckon
With water praying and call of seagull and rook
And the knock of sailing boots on the net webbed wall
Myself to set foot
That second
In the still sleeping town and set forth.

My birthday began with the water-

Birds and the birds of the winged trees flying my name
Above the farms and the white horses
And I rose
In rainy autumn
And walked abroad in a shower of all my days.
High tide and the heron dived when I took the road
Over the border
And the gates
Of the town closed as the town awoke ...

We see the leading American poet, the late ROBERT LOWELL, as he speaks about DYLAN THOMAS.

OLD DYLAN (V.O.): *Robert Lowell, the late American Poet Laureate, described the impact of Dylan in America.*

ROBERT LOWELL: *Then later he wrote poems about the war principally about bombing and these rather magical quite simple poems about childhood such as Fern Hill and poems in October. You feel he is a Welsh bard speaking for nature and often he has that power as though the trees and the water and the rocks and people all entered into his voice and birds particularly. Thomas's themes seemed to boil down to very few, I think, and one is a sort of love and death or rather an energy that killed – an energy that creates, and those seemed closely related and I remembered when I talked to him he spoke of the incredible joy of life – then in some other point in the conversation he was talking about the darkness and he wasn't feeling too well that day, but the joy seemed very real and the darkness seemed very real and neither of them – neither one seemed to exist without the other – um – and that's there and sex is very close to that and sex too is the energy that destroys and kills – I mean destroys and creates.*

Against a MONTAGE of STILLS of famous people in America, INTERCUT the photographs of the older DYLAN to the music of a jazz band – Particularly MONROE, GRABLE, CHAPLIN, MAE WEST, and scenes from GONE WITH THE WIND are chosen.

MID DYLAN (V.O.): *From his adolescence to his end, Dylan had adored the screen goddesses. He would actually meet them in Hollywood – Shelley Winters and Marilyn Monroe and Charlie Chaplin – "I pissed on the plant in your porch," he said. And all the screen images swirled through his tour of fame. As he wrote to his New York friend, Loren MacIver, he admired Betty Grable's pylons, and he asked himself:*

Is M. West a lesbian, does Bette B. hustle,
in parties out there, do the stars wear disheverly?
Did ever poor Dylan's

onslaught on silence throughout his so cleverly
agented odyssey raise any bustle ...
in the chromium homes on the Hills of Beverly,
hashish, hot splashes, nipple, nibble and nuzzle ...
Did you paint Yale and Harvard O'Hara Scarlet?
Have a bash at the deans? Did you maestro their broads
with a flash of cold mutton?

Another MONTAGE of scenes from American cities FEATURES New York and night life there.

OLD DYLAN (V.O.): *Of course, Dylan knew of his deliberate degradation of himself and his talents, once he was sent back home, sodden with liquor and with very little profit in his pocket. On his second odyssey across America, Caitlin went with him, but in their public rows and sousing, they became an embarrassment as well as a legend. After visiting Max Ernst and the last of the Surrealists, Dylan wrote a mock epitaph:*

We see copies of paintings by MAX ERNST ... C'est le Chapeau ... La Cotte d'Os.

OLD DYLAN (V.O.):   *We were killed in action, Manhattan Island,*
Spring, 1952,
in a gallant battle against American generosity.
An American called Double Rye shot Caitlin to
death.
I was scalped by a Bourbon.
Posthumous love to you ...

We MOVE from CAITLIN and DYLAN at a railroad station to him crossing the Golden Gate Bridge to San Francisco, and smiling roguishly at the end.

OLD DYLAN (V.O.): *And then back in Wales, I wrote to a dear American woman friend, regretting the beautiful West where men are sometimes men and the bars are always exultantly open.*

Again, OLD DYLAN is at his podium in the lecture hall.

MID DYLAN (V.O.): *Oh God ... What future can there be for the son of a sloth and a turnip, either I hang by my whiskery toes, thinking of nothing and lust, or sit bigheaded in the wet earth, thinking of turnip poems; and the time snails by; and San Francisco's six thousand lamenting miles away; and Wales is dead from the eisteddfodau up; and day after day I grow lazier and fatter and sadder and older and deafer and duller; gout snarls in my big toe; my children grow large and rude; I renounce my Art to make money and then make no money ... And what's a bloody poem worth – anyway. Or my play for voices, UNDER MILK WOOD?*

As OLD DYLAN recites 'And Death Shall Have No Dominion', we see photographs of DYLAN and CAITLIN and the children growing up at Laugharne, and more portraits of the ageing DYLAN, and we end up in the graveyard at Laugharne Church.

MID DYLAN (V.O.): *And death shall have no dominion.*
Dead men naked they shall be one
With the man in the wind and the west moon;
When their bones are picked clean and the clean
bones gone,
They shall have stars at elbow and foot;

Though they go mad they shall be sane,
Though they sink through the sea they shall rise again;
Though lovers be lost love shall not;
And death shall have no dominion.

And death shall have no dominion.
Under the windings of the sea
They lying long shall not die windily;
Twisting on racks when sinews give way,
Strapped to a wheel, yet they shall not break;
Faith in their hands shall snap in two,
And the unicorn evils run them through;
Split all ends up they shan't crack;
And death shall have no dominion.

And death shall have no dominion.
No more may gulls cry at their ears
Or waves break loud on the seashores;
Where blew a flower may a flower no more
Lift its head to the blows of the rain;
Though they be mad and dead as nails,
Heads of the characters hammer through daisies;
Break in the sun till the sun breaks down,
And death shall have no dominion.

During the poem, CUT AWAY to a SERIES of SHOTS of storms, and breakers crashing against cliffs, then gulls swooping above the coast of Wales, then to SEQUENCES from the film of UNDER MILK WOOD.

A pale sailor's face swims up from the dark to declare itself.

FIRST DROWNED'S VOICE: *Remember me Captain?*

CAPTAIN CAT (PETER O'TOOLE) lies back in his bunk, lost in his vision of the sea.

CAPTAIN CAT: *You're Dancing Williams!*

The first sailor looms up from the dark and is gone.

FIRST DROWNED'S VOICE: *I lost my step in Nantucket.*

Now another sailor's face swims up from the dark.

SECOND DROWNED'S VOICE: *Do you see me, Captain? The white bone talking. I'm Tom-Fred the donkeyman ... we shared the same girl once ... her name was Mrs. Probert ...*

As the face disappears, we are moving into the violet eyes of a beautiful woman sitting on a Welsh brass bed (ELIZABETH TAYLOR). The edge of the frame is grey with the gauze of memory.

ROSIE PROBERT'S VOICE: *Rosie Probert, thirty-three Duck Lane. Come on up boys, I'm dead.*

A bearded man's face now swims up from the dark.

THIRD DROWNED'S VOICE: *Hold me, Captain, I'm Jonah Jarvis, come to a bad end, very enjoyable.*

A face, dripping with water and sharp-nosed on fat shoulders tattooed with mermaids, swims forward. It laughs drunkenly.

FOURTH DROWNED'S VOICE: *Albert Pomeroy Jones, sea-lawyer, born in Mumbles, sung like a linnet, crowned you with a flagon, tattooed with mermaids, thirst like a dredger, died of blisters.*

Another bearded face of a handsome sailor now swims forward through waves of darkness.

FIRST DROWNED'S VOICE: *The skull at your earhole is ...*

FIFTH DROWNED'S VOICE: *Curly Bevan. Tell my auntie it was me that pawned the ormolu clock.*

CAPTAIN CAT smiles on his pillow.

CAPTAIN CAT: *Aye, aye, Curly.*

The Fifth Drowned Sailor now starts to sing the old sad Welsh sea-shanty 'Santiana'. As he sings, DISSOLVE backwards and forwards between CAPTAIN CAT, tears now reddening his blind eyes, and the singer and the other sailors, listening. Their song ends, and DISSOLVE back to the old weeping sea-Captain, as he starts up in his bunk.

CAPTAIN CAT: *Oh, my dead dears!*

The near-dead DYLAN is bloated and pale.

OLD DYLAN (V.O.): *In his last performances, he looked as if he was expiring.*

We see the cemetery at Laugharne and other Welsh churchyards.

OLD DYLAN (V.O.): *Dylan knew he was committing a form of suicide by fame in almost his last poem, 'Lament':*

> *Now I am a man no more no more*
> *And a black reward for a roaring life,*
> *(Sighed the old ram rod, dying of strangers),*
> *Tidy and cursed in my dove cooed room*
> *I lie down thin and hear the good bells jaw –*
> *For, oh, my soul found a Sunday wife*
> *In the coal black sky and she bore angels!*
> *Harpies around me out of her womb!*
> *Chastity pays for me, piety sings,*
> *Innocence sweetens my last black breath,*
> *Modesty hides my thighs in her wings,*
> *And all the deadly virtues plague my death!*

The lights are going out in the Main Street of Laugharne.

MID DYLAN (V.O.): *Although he could not pay his own bills for his family, Caitlin and Dylan took in his old parents at Laugharne. Dylan's 'Collected Poems' had proved to D.J. THOMAS that his son was the great poet the father had always wanted to be.*

Now a photograph of DYLAN'S father, D.J. THOMAS, appears.

MID DYLAN (V.O.): *His last words were: "It's full circle now."*

Among the gravestones in Laugharne churchyard, MID DYLAN wanders abstractedly.

MID DYLAN (V.O.): *Dylan wrote one of his greater poems on the ending of his father.*

> *Do not go gentle into that good night,*
> *Old age should burn and rave at close of day;*
> *Rage, rage against the dying of the light.*

> *Wild men who caught and sang the sun in flight,*
> *And learn, too late, they grieved it on its way,*
> *Do not go gentle into that good night.*

> *Grave men, near death, who see with blinding sight*
> *Blind eyes could blaze like meteors and be gay,*
> *Rage, rage against the dying of the light.*

(MID DYLAN sits among the tombstones.)
And you, my father, there on the sad height,
Curse, bless, me now with your fierce tears, I pray
Do not go gently into that good night.
Rage, rage, against the dying of the light.

MID DYLAN is seen from the back. FEATURE the PARK-KEEPER as he walks through the dusk in Cwmdonkin Park.

MID DYLAN (V.O.): *Dylan was still looking for his childhood as he prepared to die: "I went up into Cwmdonkin Park, the childish, lonely, remembered music fingering on in the suddenly gentle wind. Dusk was folding the Park around, like another, darker snow. Soon the bell would ring for the closing of the gates, though the Park was empty. The park-keeper walked by the reservoir, where swans had glided, on his rounds. I walked by his side and asked him my questions, up the swathed drives past buried beds and loaded utterly still furred and birdless trees towards the last gate. He said:*

We see the PARK-KEEPER backed by MID DYLAN, who remembers himself as a BOY running round the park in FLASHBACKS. They end by sitting on a bench.

PARK-KEEPER: *Oh yes, yes, I knew him well. He used to climb the reservoir railings and pelt the old swans. Run like a billygoat over the grass you should keep off of. Cut branches off the trees. Carve words on the benches. Pull up moss in the rockery, go snip through the dahlias. Fight in the bandstand. Climb the elms and moon up the top like a owl. Light fires in the bushes. Play on the green bank. Oh yes, I knew him well. I think he was happy all the time. I've known him by the thousands.*

MID DYLAN: *What has become of him now?*

(the park bell rings)

PARK-KEEPER: *Dead ... Dead ... Dead ... Dead ... Dead ... Dead.*

We now see DYLAN drinking himself to death in America and finishing in New York, where he arrived over the Brooklyn Bridge. He stayed at the Chelsea Hotel and his chosen tavern was The White Horse.

OLD DYLAN (V.O.): *On his last and fourth trip to lecture in America, Dylan had fallen into the New York habit of popping pills along with his alcohol, a deadly mixture. This was the beginning of the drug culture of Greenwich Village, the uppers and downers to add to the booze at The White Horse Tavern. To keep himself performing, Dylan was taking benzedrine and sleeping-pills, phenobarbitone and atropine. He was suffering from occasional black-outs and was being given large amounts of cortisone and morphine.*

After a drunken DYLAN shot, we see him twice with the Proprietor of The White Horse Tavern, followed by ANOTHER STILL of DYLAN with a large drink in his hand in the Greenwich Village boozer. This is the last photograph of him.

MID DYLAN (V.O.): *I've had eighteen straight whiskies. I think that's the record.*

DYLAN read UNDER MILK WOOD at the Young Women's Hebrew Association in New York.

MID DYLAN (V.O.): *At the Young Women's Hebrew Association, the dying Dylan gave a last successful reading of Under Milk Wood. Two of the actresses, Sadie Thompson and Nancy Wickwire, remembered that performance.*

We INTERCUT the interviews with STILLS of DYLAN directing the show.

SADIE THOMPSON: *We went up to the office here at the 'Y' – we all met up there – met Dylan for the first time and went into Dr. Kolodines' office and proceeded to read it and as I remember and none of us really thought that it was very readable ... He wasn't a director at all, that's really the primary thing that all of us remember – I think it's that his loving the words, savouring the words, the way he did.*

NANCY WICKWIRE: *I don't remember his ever giving us any other direction except as Celia said love the words and that was all he ever told us – it was the only thing he ever told us to do. On the last afternoon that we gave 'Under Milk Wood' when he was desperately ill, we didn't think we would be able to do the last performance because he was so ill, but he said he wanted to do it and he said he would be all right – um – the doctor gave him a shot of something and he seemed to recover. We got on our respective stools – uh – and the spotlight came on him and he was very pale and very ill and I know whatever nerves we had as actors were completely gone because we were all just so feeling for him – I think that's probably one of the greatest theatrical moments I've ever known in my life that when that light came up on him sick as he was – all the lights came on and it was the most beautiful inspiring fantastic performance he ever gave of a play.*

We see the façade of the Chelsea Hotel, then we MOVE towards a sickroom window of St Vincent's Hospital.

MID DYLAN (V.O.): *He fell ill in the Chelsea – he was taken to St Vincent's Hospital, where he died.*

We see an UNDERTAKER lying beside a purple-lined coffin.

DYLAN (V.O.): *Evans the Death drove his body back from the ship at Southampton to Laugharne.*

Over existing film and photographs of DYLAN's burial at Laugharne, we see a PRIEST and a coffin, which is put by MOURNERS in a hearse full of flowers. The MOURNERS and CAITLIN follow the hearse to the cemetery at Laugharne.

MID DYLAN (V.O.):: *Before his burial at Laugharne, Dylan in his 'Prologue' told of his love of life.*

OLD DYLAN (V.O.): *I hear the bouncing hills*
Grow larked and greener at berry brown
Fall and the dew larks sing
Taller this thunderclap spring, and how
More spanned with angels ride
The mansouled fiery islands Oh,
Holier than their eyes,
And my shining men no more alone
As I sail out to die.

The MOURNERS stand round the open grave, into which the coffin has been lowered. A service is read over the body of the dead poet.

Now we see the widow CAITLIN and her friends looking out from Laugharne Castle across the bay.

MID DYLAN (V.O.): *Other than in his poems, Dylan the Bard left behind him a play for voices, which captured the essence of sea-side Wales, forever caught between dream and heaven and earth, beauty and darkness. As Dylan's friend Richard Burton said, UNDER MILK WOOD was all about religion, sex and death.*

SEQUENCES from the film of UNDER MILK WOOD.

The mittened fingers of the old CAPTAIN CAT feel with love a scrimshaw whaling scene on a walrus tooth. PULL BACK to show him with his memories in his cabin in Schooner House on the quayside of the sea-town.

SECOND VOICE (RYAN DAVIES) V.O.: *Captain Cat, at his window thrown wide to the sun and the clippered seas he sailed long ago ...*

In a dive bar, the young CAPTAIN CAT stands, his eyes large and blue, his beard black, a gold ring in his ear. By his side, a lout. The lout picks a fight, the young CAT throws beer in his face, the lout pulls a knife, the young CAT breaks a bottle as a weapon, then kicks the lout down through a bar screen.

All of CAT's dreams are gauzed with memory.

SECOND VOICE: ... *When his eyes were blue and bright, slumbers and voyages; ear-ringed and rolling, I Love You Rosie Probert tattooed on his belly, he brawls with broken bottles in the fug and babel of the dark dock bars ...*

Now the young CAT leans over the bar to kiss a henna-red barmaid, while his hand gropes at the breasts of a cuffing mulatress.

SECOND VOICE: ... *Roves with a herd of short and good time cows in every naughty port and twines and souses with the drowned and blowzy-breasted dead.*

Now we are in the bedroom of ROSIE PROBERT (ELIZABETH TAYLOR), where she sits on her quilt on her brass bed, looking up with her eyes like violet moons.

ROSIE turns towards the bedhead, stretching an arm.

ROSIE PROBERT: *Tom Cat ... Tom Cat ...*

SECOND VOICE: *One voice of all he remembers dearly as his dream buckets down. Lazy early Rosie ...*

We move across to the bedhead, where the young CAT is climbing over the brass rail, pulling off his sea-boots as he comes.

He falls into the laughing arms of ROSIE.

SECOND VOICE: *In that gulf and haven, fleets by the dozen have anchored for the little heaven of the night ...*

A hilltop by the Druid circle of ancient stones, overlooking the dawn sea and the harbour and the town. There the FIRST VOICE stands alone. The dream music fades. There is silence.

FIRST VOICE (RICHARD BURTON): *Time passes. Listen. Time passes. An owl flies home past Bethesda, to a chapel in an oak. And the dawn inches up.*

PAN along the distant quayside, showing the whole length of Cockle Row with the hills of Wales beyond.

FIRST VOICE: *Stand on this hill. This is Llaregyb Hill. Old as the hills, high, cool, and green, and from this small circle of stones, made by the Druids for a come-to-visit Milk Wood ...*

As we PAN round the view below and past the Druid stones, the FIRST VOICE mysteriously is found standing again on the far side of the stones.

FIRST VOICE: ... *You can see all the town below you sleeping in the first of the dawn.*

On a sea headland of grass and yellow gorse, MAE ROSE COTTAGE (SUSAN PENHALIGON) sits among her goats, pulling at the petals of a flower.

MAE ROSE COTTAGE: *He loves me, he loves me not*
He loves me, he loves me not ...

In his dinghy, the Zanzibar, NOGOOD BOYO (DAVID JASON) lies on his back, dreaming, a fishing line tied to his foot. There is a sudden tug on the line. NOGOOD bends his leg until he can get a hand on the line to pull it in. At the end of the line is a corset.

NOGOOD BOYO: *Bloody funny fish!*

He puts the corset down in the boat as his pillow, and lies back in a day-dream. Skiffle music sounds.

Out of the waves emerges MRS. DAI BREAD TWO (RUTH MADOC), wearing only a bangle on her wrist. She stretches up her arms and her breasts.

In the Zanzibar, NOGOOD holds out the dripping corset.

NOGOOD BOYO: *Would you like this nice wet corset, Mrs. Dai Bread Two?*

Now in NOGOOD's dream again, the hard and laughing MRS. DAI BREAD TWO is covered with shining scales of armour, while NOGOOD himself wades into the sea, offering her the corset.

NOGOOD BOYO: *Would you like this nice corset, Mrs. Dai Bread ...*

MRS. DAI BREAD TWO: *No, I won't!*

NOGOOD BOYO: *And a bite of my apple?*

Screaming with glee, MRS. DAI BREAD TWO pulls NOGOOD down into her cold and scaly embrace, as the camera and the music tilt up and swell to show the two in a great sweep of bay and sea.

On the sea headland in the evening, MAE ROSE COTTAGE has undone her blouse and is drawing circles of lipstick round her nipples.

Beyond her, a bearded nannygoat champs and sneers. She goes on drawing scarlet circles round her nipples.

MAE ROSE COTTAGE: *I'm fast. I'm a bad lot. God will strike me dead. I'm seventeen. I'll go to hell.*

The small white kid passes her, flicking its ears, not caring. She pushes out her breasts with her hands to make them bigger.

MAE ROSE COTTAGE: *You just wait. I'll sin till I blow up!*

She turns round to the sneering nannygoat.

MAE ROSE COTTAGE: *Oh you go home!*

FIRST VOICE: *The thin night darkens. The breeze from the creased water sighs the streets close ...*

In the dark wood, RICHARD BURTON as the FIRST VOICE smiles secretly, seems to cross himself, and moves off.

FIRST VOICE: *... Under Milk waking Wood.*

Now on the crest of the hill under the dark trees of the wood, we see the black shapes of the FIRST and SECOND VOICES going into the night.

In the overgrown graveyard, the SECOND VOICE has fallen on a tombstone. The FIRST VOICE helps him to his feet. They hear the noise of the chapel door opening, and they move away.

The REVEREND ELI JENKINS (AUBREY RICHARDS) comes out of Bethesda chapel, and walks down the path in front of it, looking round at the night trees.

ELI JENKINS: *Milk Wood on the hill, the memorial of peoples that dwelt in the region of Llaregyb before the Celts left the Land of Summer and where the old wizards made themselves ...*

The REVEREND JENKINS catches sight of someone in the wood, and we see ... A photograph of YOUNG DYLAN and CAITLIN. They are radiant and smiling in Wales for the first time together.

ELI JENKINS (V.O.): *... A wife out of flowers.*

We hear a Welsh folk-song, plaintive and haunting. And we see the beauty of the hill farms of Wales. Above the song we also hear the last verse of 'Fern Hill'.

OLD DYLAN (V.O.): *Nothing I cared, in the lamb white days, that*
time would take me
Up to the swallow thronged loft by the shadow of my hand,
In the moon that is always rising,
Nor that riding to sleep
I should hear him fly with the high fields
And wake to the farm forever fled from the childless land.
Oh as I was young and easy in the mercy of his means ...
Time held me green and dying
Though I sang in my chains like the sea.

Now we FADE into a view of DYLAN'S grave at Laugharne, then into a final sunset over the sea.

MID DYLAN (V.O.): *In Welsh, Dylan meant the Son of the Wave. He sings to us forever.*